ADVANCE PRAISE

". . . sprinkled with scripture, Don and Bonnie encourage their readers to follow the Bible. Their conversational tone feels like they are speaking right to me. Their strong Christian ministry and their ability to share personal stories made me want to keep reading. Be inspired by reading this book . . .

I was!"

— Joan McConville,
Regional Staff Associate,
Saddleback Laguna Woods

Your Heart is an Open Book

Finding Answers in God's Word

DON AND BONNIE SENNOTT

Your Heart is an Open Book: Finding Answers in God's Word
Published by BECAUSE HE LOVES US PRESS
Trabuco Canyon, California

ISBN: 978-0-578-64569-8

RELIGION / Christian Living / Family & Relationships
RELIGION / Christian Living / Inspirational

QUANTITY PURCHASES:
Schools, companies, professional groups, clubs, and other organizations may qualify for special terms when ordering quantities of this title. For information, email don@becausehelovesuspress.com.

Because He Loves Us Press

This book is printed in the United States of America.

All Bible verses are cited courtesy of www.biblegateway.com.

DEDICATION

This book is dedicated to the people whose encouragement, chastening, comforting, and love have helped us on our journey to find a closer relationship with God.

TABLE OF CONTENTS

ABBREVIATION LIST

In this book, the abbreviation for the translation (i.e. NIV, NLT, etc.) denotes the first use of a translation in a subsection. Consecutive entries in the subsection from the same translation do not carry an abbreviation. Whenever the translation being used changes, the verse where the change occurs will be notated.

The Amplified Bible . . . . AMP

The Contemporary English Version . . . . CEV

The International Children's Bible . . . . .ICB

King James Version . . . . .KJV

Mounce Reverse-Interlinear New Testament . . . . . . .MOUNCE

New American Standard Bible® . . . . NASB

New English Translation . . . . NET

New International Version® . . . . NIV

New King James Version . . . . NKJV

New Living Translation . . . . NLT

The Message . . . . MESSAGE

The Living Bible . . . . TLB

The Passion Translation . . . . TPT

OPENING THOUGHTS

YOU WILL KEEP IN PERFECT PEACE ALL WHO TRUST IN YOU,
ALL WHOSE THOUGHTS ARE FIXED ON YOU!

Isaiah 26:3 (NLT)

ABOUT THE TITLE OF THIS BOOK

We didn't select the title *Your Heart is an Open Book*; it selected us. During our morning devotionals, Bonnie was reading Psalm 139 in The Passion Translation when she stopped at the line, *You read my heart like an open book.*

"Your heart is an open book," she said. "Isn't that what this book is all about?"

You are so intimately aware of me, Lord.
You read my heart like an open book
and you know all the words I'm about to speak
before I even start a sentence!
You know every step I will take before my journey even begins.
You've gone into my future to prepare the way,
and in kindness you follow behind me
to spare me from the harm of my past.
With your hand of love upon my life,
you impart a blessing to me.

Psalm 139:3-5 (TPT)

To God, all of our hearts are open books. Yet, we often get so hung up trying to edit past chapters that we fail to find the joys available to us when we dare, with God's help, to write new chapters.

God's heart is also an open book. He gave us His Word as His biography. The more we get to know Him, the more we will come to love him. The more we love Him, the more we'll want to share His love with others. Shouldn't it be the goal of every Christian to have the "open book of their heart" a volume God is delighted to read?

"You have done well, and proven yourself to be my loyal and trustworthy servant." Matthew 25:21b

Blessings,
Your friends in Christ,
Don & Bonnie

"If Only I Could See the Lord"

"If only I could see the Lord," I heard a skeptic say,
"or hear His voice or feel his touch my doubts would melt away.
Like Thomas, I would call him Lord, if I could see his scars;
until I do, I'll doubt he's true, my faith is in the stars.

Just then he heard a soft voice say, "Look in, not up, my friend.
The stars you trust were less than dust until I put them there.
My Word gave life to everything; My death gave life to all.
My light dispels the darkest night and frees man from the fall.

"And though you never see the wind, nor hear the dark of night,
you'll feel my awesome presence when you step into my light.
Child, if you want to feel my scars and see me face-to-face,
you'll need to find me in your heart, my special hiding place."

I will bless the Lord who guides me; even at night my heart instructs me.

PSALM 16:7

SHARING GOD'S LOVE

In the 5th grade, I had to write a long report for English class. Way back then (1959), we didn't have computers or iPads. You scratched out your report on a pad of paper, then tackled the arduous task of typing it on your old Underwood. It took longer for me to "hunt and peck" my way through typing the report than it had taken to write it. When finished, I was certain I had an A+ paper, so I went downstairs to show it to my Mom and Dad.

As I entered the dining room, my older sister Pat snatched the pages from my hand. "What's this?" she said, waving the report in front of my face.

"Give me that," I shrieked, as I reached out for my report. The combination of my grabbing and her twisting to get away resulted in my report being torn and mangled. My A+ paper was suddenly an F-minus! I stomped off to my room, knowing I'd never make it out of the 5th grade.

The next morning, as I was preparing to go to school, I noticed a neatly typed document on top of my books. My father, it turned out, had stayed up late into the night retyping my report. Today, I can look back on that episode as an example of a father's love.

In this book, we look back on experiences we've had, on sermons we've listened to, and on stories we have read that bring to mind the love our Father in heaven has for us. We also look at ways we can come into a closer relationship with God through Jesus Christ.

God gives us His love so we can give it to others who, in turn, give it to others.

Let us think of ways to motivate one another to acts of love and good works. Hebrews 10:24 (NLT)

You might ask, "Aren't you simply putting a new label on the old 'faith without works is dead' argument of the apostle James?" Our response would be that true faith is evidenced by works motivated by love. Sharing God's love is not doing things to earn His love; it is doing things in response to God's love. It is blessing others as we have been blessed.

God's love is wonderfully contagious. The more we spread it around the more we feel it growing in our lives.

You will notice we use a generous number of Scriptures. Sharing God's love starts with discovering God's heart. The best place to discover God's heart is in God's Word.

As you read these pages, you will encounter God's Word as presented in several translations. We are not Bible scholars; we are two people who love the Lord, and who pray the Holy Spirit will guide us as we try to apply His Word in our lives.

Recognizing that God's love is a gift we are to share with others has changed our lives. Our hope is that it will change your life, too.

Love Fulfills God's Requirements

Owe nothing to anyone—except for your obligation to love one another. If you love your neighbor, you will fulfill the requirements of God's law.

ROMANS 13:8 (NLT)

THE OLIVE WOOD CROSS

A few years ago, Bonnie's friend Barb gave her a hand-held olive wood cross from Israel. Bonnie was so touched by the gift that she asked me to see if we could get a few crosses to give away. That gift from Barb became the catalyst for us to share God's love in a new way.

Here's how it works: Bonnie carries a couple of crosses in her purse. When a server in a restaurant or a clerk in a shop is especially kind or helpful, Bonnie leaves the normal tip, then she presents them with a velvet bag with the cross inside, saying, "I have a gift I'd like to give you. You have been so kind, I'm guessing you are a Christian."

Many say, "Yes." Others say, "I'm Catholic," to which Bonnie responds, "You believe in Jesus; that's all that matters to me." Of course, a few decline the gift saying they aren't Christian, to whom Bonnie says, "You may keep it to share with a Christian friend if you'd like."

But in your hearts revere Christ as Lord. Always be prepared to give an answer to everyone who asks you to give the reason for the hope that you have. But do this with gentleness and respect. 1 Peter 3:15 (NIV)

We make frequent visits to Kaiser Healthcare. You'd be surprised how many doctors and nurses are Christian. Occasionally we see a patient who is going through a particularly rough patch. A kind word and the gift of the cross can give comfort to someone who may otherwise feel frightened and alone.

He himself bore our sins in his body on the cross, so that we might die to sins and live for righteousness; "by his wounds you have been healed." 1 Peter 2:24

Sometimes Bonnie will give someone an extra cross suggesting, "You will know who to give this to." In one instance, Bonnie had given an extra cross to a hairstylist. When a client told her she had been severely depressed, the stylist prayed with her and gave her the cross. When the client returned several weeks later, she hugged the stylist and said, "Your love and that cross saved my life. I was going to commit suicide, but I held that cross and prayed."

There is no special power in the small hand-held crosses themselves; the power is in Jesus. The crosses offer a way to share our love with people we may only have a few moments with.

Maybe you have been looking for a new way to share your love. The beauty of the crosses from Israel is, thanks to Amazon, you don't have to travel to Jerusalem to get them. If you type "olive wood holding cross" in the Amazon search bar, you will see a variety of crosses to choose from.

Another way to share God's love is to send uplifting greeting cards or "I am praying for you" texts or emails. You never know when the Holy Spirit will move you to reach out to someone. Whether you hand someone a wooden cross, send them a greeting card, or simply show your Christianity with a hug or a smile, you may encourage them to think about God's love for them.

> *As a result of your ministry, they will give glory to God. For your generosity to them and to all believers will prove that you are obedient to the Good News of Christ. 2*
>
> CORINTHIANS 9:13 (NLT)

THE SKUNK IN THE PRAYER ROOM

Have you ever felt like the skunk in the prayer room—that person everyone else looks at with destain when they suggest showing special kindness to or praying for someone the group is convinced doesn't deserve kindness or prayers?

Of course, Jesus' words in Matthew remind us everyone deserves prayer, and you might encourage the group to pray, "Lord, we do not have compassion for the person we have been asked to pray for, but we know you do. Please help him."

But I tell you, love your enemies and pray for those who persecute you, that you may be children of your Father in heaven. He causes his sun to rise on the evil and the good, and sends rain on the righteous and the unrighteous. Matthew 5:44-45 (NIV)

After church one Sunday, we were sitting in a fast-food restaurant when another customer started complaining quite loudly to one of the workers that his order was wrong. "I ordered two burgers, not one!" he shouted. "I just want my son to enjoy his sandwich."

The worker looked at the receipt, then explained, "The person taking the order obviously miss-heard your order, I can get you a second burger if you'll pay for it."

Still frustrated by the confusion, the man responded harshly, "Just forget it. We'll make do."

"I wonder if I should give him one of our olive-wood crosses?" Bonnie asked. "I think his son has a neurological disorder of some type. I can't begin to imagine how difficult it must be to raise a special needs child."

"I'm not sure this is the best time," I replied.

Following our meal, Bonnie excused herself to go to the Ladies Room. As she returned to our table, she stopped to speak to the father. "I have a gift I'd like to give you."

She pulled one of the crosses from its red velvet bag and handed it to him. "Whenever I feel tired, or hurt, or afraid, it helps me. There is no 1-800 number; it is a gift."

A smile filled his face, as the man thanked her for her kindness. Bonnie returned to our table. Almost immediately, the aggrieved worker, who happens to be a friend of ours, raced to our table. "Do you know him? He was so rude to me!"

"Yes, I know, but I felt he needed to know that God loves him. He has his hands full taking care of his son."

"That's no excuse. He is just horrible," she said, as she walked away.

A short time later, the man and his son paused as they passed our table. The father said, "Thank you" and left. The son lingered, as if wanting to say something, then followed his father out the door.

Later, when we spoke about the incident, Bonnie said she had gone to the Ladies Room to pray. "I wanted to give him one of our crosses, but I had knee-knocking fear that he would take his anger out on me. When I prayed, I got one of those 'Yes, my child' messages that let me know I wasn't the one making the decision."

"Courage is fear that has said its prayers"
Dorothy Bernard

Sharing God's love won't always make others happy. Sometimes we will end up being "the skunk in the prayer room" that God uses to spread the sweet aroma of the knowledge of Jesus.

But thanks be to God, who always leads us as captives in Christ's triumphal procession and uses us to spread the aroma of the knowledge of him everywhere.

2 CORINTHIANS 2:14

BASEBALL AND BIBLES

God truly works in mysterious ways. April 8, 1974, I unexpectedly found myself in Atlanta on a business trip. I walked into the Howard Johnson adjacent to Fulton County Stadium and asked the desk clerk for a room.

"Are you kidding?" he said. "Everything is sold out around here."

Just then the phone rang. I listened as the clerk took a cancellation. "I guess I have a room for you after all."

"Do you think I'll be able to get tickets to tonight's Braves game," I asked.

"Not likely. The game is sold out."

A woman who was standing in the lobby approached me with her young daughter. "My husband is caught in a business meeting and won't be able to make it in time for the game. Would you like his ticket?"

I offered to pay her, but since the ticket didn't cost her anything, she said she wouldn't feel right selling it. I thanked her and headed for the stadium. That evening, I was one of 53,775 people who showed up for the game—a Braves attendance record—to see Hank Aaron hit home run #715, breaking Babe Ruth's record.

At that time in my life, I didn't read the Bible regularly. But returning to my hotel room following the game, something moved me to open the Gideon Bible that was on the desk. I started to read the following story in the book of Acts:

Eutychus Raised from the Dead at Troas

On the first day of the week we came together to break bread. Paul spoke to the people and, because he intended to leave the next day, kept on talking until midnight. There were many lamps in the upstairs room where we were meeting. Seated in a window was a young man named Eutychus, who was sinking into a deep sleep as Paul talked on and on. When he was sound asleep, he fell to the ground from the third story and was picked up dead. Paul went down, threw himself on the young man and put his arms around him. "Don't be alarmed," he said. "He's alive!" Then he went upstairs again and broke bread and ate. After talking until daylight, he left. The people took the young man home alive and were greatly comforted. Acts 20:7-12 (NIV)

That story tickled my funny bone. I thought about the many times I had grumbled about a preacher giving sermons that were too long, but this was a case where someone was actually "preached to death." The story of Eutychus made me wonder if there were other stories in the Bible I had missed. That night something changed for me. I read on for several hours, and the more I read, the more I wanted to read.

What some call coincidences others call God's providence. I happened to be in the right place at the right time. A generous woman had an extra ticket to the game. Dodger pitcher Al Downing decided to pitch to Aaron rather than walk him. A Gideon's Bible was left in that hotel room where I could see it. My random choice of which Scripture to read was the story from Acts 20. Just an interesting series of coincidences, or was God winking at me?

Psalm 119 contains 176 verses that extol the Word of God, the most familiar being verse 105: *Your word is a lamp for my feet, a light on my path.* Many of the verses of this psalm have to do with the psalmist's desire to follow the word of God. I, like the psalmist, have found God's Word to be a lamp unto my feet, a light on my path. I am thankful the lamp started to burn so much brighter for me one miraculous evening in Atlanta. It is our hope that you too will fall in love with God's Word.

JESUS LOVES YOU

You sing the song "Jesus Loves Me," but do you really believe he loves YOU?

Sometimes things are so familiar that we miss the truth: they apply to us, too. One of the most familiar verses in the Bible is John 3:16 (NIV): "*For God so loved the world that he gave his one and only Son that whoever believes in him shall not perish but have eternal life.*" Do you really accept that YOU are part of the world that Christ died for, or do you secretly wish God would help you internalize that life-giving truth?

A while back, Bonnie was longing to hear God's voice. "I know he loves everybody else," she confessed. "But I want to know He loves ME."

A few days later, we attended a church service. The pastor, Buddy Owen, approached the pulpit, paused for a moment, then began, "Someone here tonight wants to know God loves THEM. I'm here to tell you he does!"

With a smile on his face he added, "If you're that person, you may leave now."

Bonnie turned to me with her radiant smile and asked, "Should we go?"

It turns out, Bonnie isn't the only one who wonders about God's love for them. The following Sunday, our neighbors knocked on our door excited to tell us about something that happened during their church service.

"Our head pastor was on vacation, so the assistant pastor gave the sermon. He began to tell us he had a very troubling week, and he started to question God's love for him.

"'Then,' he said, 'I saw a white Prius with a license plate which completely changed my attitude.'"

My neighbor continued, "The two video screens on each side of the platform were filled with the image of Bonnie's license plate.

"The pastor explained, 'To anyone else, the license plate offered the message, Jesus loves ewe (you). It was far more meaningful to me; my initials are E.W.E! I was reminded that Jesus specifically loves Edward W. Ewart.'"

Do you know that Jesus loves you? No doubt about it?

God speaks in a myriad of ways. He may use the words of a sermon, a license plate, the counsel of a friend—maybe even this book— to help you know that Jesus truly does love You!

> *I pray that from his glorious, unlimited resources he will empower you with inner strength through his Spirit. Then Christ will make his home in your hearts as you trust in him. Your roots will grow down into God's love and keep you strong.*

EPHESIANS 3:16-17 (NLT)

YOU FEED THEM

> *That evening the disciples came to him and said, "This is a remote place, and it's already getting late. Send the crowds away so they can go to the villages and buy food for themselves."*
>
> *But Jesus said, "That isn't necessary—you feed them."*
>
> *"But we have only five loaves of bread and two fish!" they answered.*
>
> *"Bring them here," he said. Then he told the people to sit down on the grass. Jesus took the five loaves and two fish, looked up toward heaven, and blessed them. Then, breaking the loaves into pieces, he gave the bread to the disciples, who distributed it to the people. They all ate as much as they wanted, and afterward, the disciples picked up twelve baskets of leftovers. About 5,000 men were fed that day, in*

addition to all the women and children! Matthew 14:15-21 (NLT)

If you want to get a picture of the heart of Jesus, you need only look at the story of the feeding of the five thousand. Jesus had just learned his cousin and dear friend John the Baptist had been beheaded by Herod. With a heavy heart, he had sought a place of solitude, but a large crowd followed him.

Jesus could have turned the boat around and sought a better place to mourn. Instead, he chose to step out of the boat. We see his compassion in the way he walked into the crowd and healed the sick. His pain was secondary to their pain.

Of course, Jesus could have made a cameo appearance, healed a few, and excused himself. But the crowd had come to hear him, and he wasn't going to disappoint them.

It was evening when the disciples cautioned him that the crowd would be getting hungry. Perhaps, he should send them away so they could buy food for themselves. The disciples were no doubt stunned when Jesus said, "You feed them."

I can just imagine Jesus asking, "What do we have that we can share with them?" Jesus has the heart of a provider, and like all good providers, he found the way. "Five loaves and two fish? No problem!"

We also see Jesus' heart of gratitude. He blessed the food, giving thanks to the Father for the abundance. We also learn from this story that God isn't a God of minimums. Everyone ate their fill and there were plenty of leftovers.

Sometimes, when I read this story, I wonder what the disciples did with the leftovers. There is a group called Feeding America that knows what to do with leftovers. They gather groceries that have reached their sell-by date from local merchants and distribute them to local food banks. Supported by donors, the Feeding America nationwide network of food banks secures and distributes 4.3

billion meals each year through food pantries and meal programs throughout the United States.

If you would like to support efforts to end hunger in America, a list of food banks that would appreciate donations or volunteers can be found at https://www.feedingamerica.org/find-your-local-foodbank.

MORE JOY-FILLED TOMORROW

Should we just forget about the past, or should we hold onto memories of past relationships? The answer depends on just how memories of those relationships affect you. People often miss opportunities for joy in their lives because they are preoccupied with shadow-boxing with their past. They carry grudges and grievances for things that happened a long time ago, and memories can become terrible slave masters if we let them. The good news is that you can open a new chapter in the book of your heart and pave the way to a more joy-filled tomorrow.

Pastor Rich Warren suggested some steps we can take:

Ask God to help you move past the hurt.

You may recall the story of Joseph and his coat of many colors. Sold into slavery by his brothers, Joseph could have let the pain of his abuse color his feeling about his brothers. Instead, he chose to move past the hurt and show them grace.

His brothers then came and threw themselves down before him. "We are your slaves," they said.

But Joseph said to them, "Don't be afraid. Am I in the place of God? You intended to harm me, but God intended it for good." Genesis 50:18-20 (NIV)

Give God time to work on you.

Wait patiently for the Lord. Be brave and courageous. Yes, wait patiently for the Lord. Psalm 27:14 (NLT)

Seek God's answers from the best self-help book ever written: the Bible.

For the word of God is alive and powerful. It is sharper than the sharpest two-edged sword, cutting between soul and spirit, between joint and marrow. It exposes our innermost thoughts and desires. Hebrews 4:12

Choose love over resentment or retaliation.

"So now I am giving you a new commandment: Love each other. Just as I have loved you, you should love each other. Your love for one another will prove to the world that you are my disciples." John 13:34-35

Be willing to take the first step.

"But when you are praying, first forgive anyone you are holding a grudge against, so that your Father in heaven will forgive your sins, too." Mark 11:25

Be kind and compassionate to one another, forgiving each other, just as in Christ God forgave you. Ephesians 4:32 (NIV)

Choose to look at things from a different perspective.

Try to put yourself in the position of a neutral observer. Ask the question, "Am I seeing the whole picture?"

Get the truth and never sell it; also get wisdom, discipline, and good judgment. Proverbs 23:23 (NLT)

Pride ends in humiliation, while humility brings honor. Proverbs 29:23

Find a reason to laugh.

Ecclesiastes 3:4 (AMP) tells us that there is *a time to weep, and a time to laugh; a time to mourn, and a time to dance.*

Laughing has significant health benefits. It releases endorphins in the brain that can help mood change, release tension, and even burn extra calories.

Be willing to change.

When we are cursed, we bless; when we are persecuted, we endure it; when we are slandered, we answer kindly. 1 Corinthians 4:12b, 13a (NIV)

You don't have to justify your hurt or pain. God knows.

Billy Graham once said, "Puppy love isn't real, but it is to the puppy."

Emotional scars heal slowly, but we serve a God who will help us deal with all kinds of pain.

Going forward, we offer you this prayer: May the God of hope fill you with all joy and peace as you trust in him, so that you may overflow with hope by the power of the Holy Spirit.

ROMANS 15:13 (NIV)

YOU CAN HAVE AN IMPACT

A NEW COMMAND I GIVE YOU: LOVE ONE ANOTHER.
AS I HAVE LOVED YOU, SO YOU MUST LOVE ONE ANOTHER.
BY THIS EVERYONE WILL KNOW THAT YOU ARE MY DISCIPLES,
IF YOU LOVE ONE ANOTHER.

John 13:34-35 (NIV)

FOOTPRINTS ON THE SANDS OF TIME

One of our favorite poems is "A Psalm of Life" by Henry Wadsworth Longfellow (1807-1882). We particularly like the following verses:

> *Lives of great men all remind us*
> *We can make our lives sublime,*
> *And, departing, leave behind us*
> *Footprints on the sands of time*
>
> *Footprints, that perhaps another,*
> *Sailing o'er life's solemn main,*
> *A forlorn and shipwrecked brother,*
> *Seeing, shall take heart again.*
>
> *Let us, then, be up and doing,*
> *With a heart for any fate;*
> *Still achieving, still pursuing,*
> *Learn to labor and to wait.*

When the poet writes, "we can make our lives sublime," he is telling us we can raise our lives to a level with which nothing can compare, and which is beyond all possibility of calculation, measurement or imitation.

In the 6th Chapter of Galatians, Saint Paul wrote, *Let us not become weary in doing good, for at the proper time we will reap a harvest if we do not give up. Therefore, as we have opportunity, let us do good to all people, especially to those who belong to the family of believers.* Galatians 6:9-10 (NIV)

Both the Poem by Longfellow and the writings of Saint Paul remind us that the impact we have in life depends on our willingness to persevere in doing good. Perseverance can be defined as steady persistence in a course of action, as pursuing a purpose despite difficulties, obstacles, or discouragement. Perseverance can be either good or bad depending on the motivation of the one who persists.

We can see examples of perseverance in the lives of William Wilberforce, Billy Graham, Peter Marshall, Mother Theresa, Martin Luther King, Jr., and others. These heroes of the faith lived by the words *You need to persevere so that when you have done the will of God, you will receive what he has promised.* Hebrews 10:36

We can take comfort in the fact Hebrews 10:36 doesn't say, "Only heroes of the faith who do great things will receive what God has promised." The verse says *You need to persevere so that when you have done the will of God you will receive what he has promised.* So, when we, that means you and me, do the will of God, we will receive what he has promised.

And what is the will of God? Jesus tells us in John 6:40, "*For my Father's will is that everyone who looks to the Son and believes in him shall have eternal life, and I will raise him up at the last day.*" Jesus is speaking about a belief that changes the heart.

The prophet Jeremiah explained what God is looking for in His people: *I, the LORD, search the heart, I test the mind, Even to give every man according to his ways, According to the fruit of his doings.* Jeremiah 17:10 (NKJV)

Which brings us once again to those footprints we are leaving on the sands of time. The book *Random Acts of Kindness* by Dete Meserve and Rachael Greco features stories and quotations which encourage the reader to look for opportunities to serve others. Often, it's the little things we do for others that end up being our most lasting footprints.

As you go through this week, we encourage you to look for opportunities to share God's love, keeping the words of missionary C.T. Studd in mind: "We've only one life; 'twill soon be past. Only what's done for Christ will last."

"Then the righteous will answer him, 'Lord, when did we see you hungry and feed you, or thirsty and give you something to drink? When did we see you a stranger and invite you in, or needing clothes and clothe you? When did we see you sick or in prison and go to visit you?'

"The King will reply, 'Truly I tell you, whatever you did for one of the least of these brothers and sisters of mine, you did for me.'"

MATTHEW 25:37-40 (NIV)

TWO PORTIAS

Have you ever returned to your old neighborhood to thank a neighbor, a teacher, a church member, or a boss whose kindness, chastening, or generosity had a positive impact on your life? Several years ago, I decided to take a bouquet of flowers to my sixth-grade teacher, Mrs. Ware. I looked up her address and visited her home in Northwest Washington, D.C.

Mrs. Ware was one of those teachers who could bring out the best in her students. She had her hands full when it came to young Donnie Sennott; I was bored with school, unwilling to study, and angry because, as a minority, I was tolerated, not embraced by most of the other students. Mrs. Ware was Afro-American, but she treated all of her students with kindness. Her tool for converting me from an intransigent problem-child to a student who loves learning was a cardboard model of the Potomac Electric Power Company generating plant.

One afternoon, she asked me to stay after the class was dismissed. "Donnie, she said, "I have a project I need your help with. We are going to be studying electricity next week, and I would like you to assemble this model of the powerplant down by the river."

She lowered her voice and said, "This is a difficult task, and I need someone smart like you to do it." I had never considered myself smart, but if Mrs. Ware thought I was smart, I'd do my best to prove her right. Today, I realize that anyone in the class could have handled that simple task. She chose me because giving me the project was her way of sharing God's love with someone who needed it.

Fast forward to the day of my visit to her home. I rang the doorbell. After a few moments, the door opened and a woman not much older than me greeted me with a broad smile.

"Is Mrs.Ware home, Mrs. Portia Ware?" I asked.

With a puzzled look on her face, she replied, "I am Portia Ware."

"But you can't be!" I said. "Mrs. Ware was much older than me."

"You are speaking of my mother. She recently went to be with the Lord."

I offered my condolences, handed her the flowers, and started to tell her how important her mother had been to me. She invited me in, told me how much my visit helped her, and we spent about an hour looking at pictures and sharing our life stories.

When I shared this story with Bonnie, she told me about Mr. Cox, one of her High School teachers. She ran into him a few years after graduation. "He was just as kind and complimentary during that meeting as he had been in class," she recalled.

Looking for a way to share God's love? Take time to thank someone who helped you become what you are today.

We ought always to thank God for you, brothers and sisters,
and rightly so, because your faith is growing more and more,
and the love all of you have for one another is increasing.

2 THESSALONIANS 1:3

ADDING TO YOUR LEGACY

Nothing causes one to examine one's life quite like attending a memorial service for a friend whose life was worthy of emulation. Patricia Boss Lawrence was such a person. At her memorial, family and friends spoke of a woman who lived as if the words of Etienne de Grellet served as her life compass.

"I shall pass this way but once; any good that I can do or any kindness I can show to any human being; let me do it now. Let me not defer nor neglect it, for I shall not pass this way again." Etienne de Grellet (1773-1855)

Pat was an educator, a teacher of teachers, who, associates say left her mark on thousands of children. One close friend put it this way, "Pat had the ability to entice the best out of everybody."

"Specificity and clarity should be your goal," Pat would say. "Look someone in the eye and focus on what they are saying, not on what your next question might be."

Pat was a mother and a businesswoman; she started a consulting business at age 72, after retiring from teaching. Pat was also an adventurer, with travels that took her from a hike in the Himalayas to a bike ride in South Africa, from a climb at Machu Pichu to a 40-mile trek following the path Jesus took from Jerusalem to Capernaum.

A devout Catholic, Pat served and supported her local parish. For five years she was a docent at Christ Cathedral in Garden Grove, California. Her love for children was seen in the mission trips she took to Mexico and South Africa, where she worked to educate the poor.

Pat had boundless energy. She packed a lot of living into her 82 years. She ran the race God had marked out for her.

Therefore, since we are surrounded by such a great cloud of witnesses, let us throw off everything that hinders and the sin that so easily entangles. And let us run with perseverance the race marked out for us. Hebrews 12:1 (NIV)

With all her adventures and accomplishments, I was certain Pat's page on Wikipedia would make interesting reading. What I found was one simple line: The page for "Patricia Boss Lawrence" does not exist. Besides an obituary in a local paper and possibly a memorial service attended by a small group of family and friends, our earthly legacy will be the impact we had on others.

Want a way to add to your legacy? Jesus gave us the way: *A new command I give you: Love one another. As I have loved you, so you must love one another. By this everyone will know that you are my disciples, if you love one another.* John 13:34-35

In 1st John 3:18, we learn that loving involves action, not just words. *Dear children, let's not merely say that we love each other; let us show the truth by our actions.* 1 John 3:18 (NLT)

Each day offers fresh opportunities to add to our legacy by sharing God's love. As Pat Lawrence did, let your loving actions show you are a disciple of Christ.

> *Live a life filled with love, following the example of Christ. He loved us[a] and offered himself as a sacrifice for us, a pleasing aroma to God.*
>
> EPHESIANS 5:2

FOR SUCH A TIME AS THIS

In the book of Esther, we read about a young Jewish girl who became queen of Persia. When Haman, one of King Xerxes advisors, devised a plot to slaughter all the Jews in the kingdom, Esther was encouraged by her uncle to plead the case of the Jews before the king.

Hesitant at first, Esther sent the following reply to her uncle, "*All the king's officials and even the people in the provinces know that anyone who appears before the king in his inner court without being invited is doomed to die unless the king holds out his gold scepter. And the king has not called for me to come to him for thirty days."* Esther 4:11 (NLT)

Her uncle responded, *"If you keep quiet at a time like this, deliverance and relief for the Jews will arise from some other place, but you and your relatives will die. Who knows if perhaps you were made queen for just such a time as this?"* Esther 4:14

Esther did go to the king, identified her uncle as the man who had once saved the king's life and exposed Haman's plot. Haman and his entire family were executed, and the Jewish people were saved. Jews celebrate Esther's story during the Feast of Purim.

It is unlikely you will be called upon to save a nation, but there may be a time when you are the answer to someone's prayer. Perhaps you were made for such a time as this.

Bonnie once served as Chairman of the Board for an international self-help group. When she first joined, she had been so afraid she would make a mistake that she was reluctant to even make coffee. A few years later, having advanced in the organization, she found herself about to speak before the members about a delicate subject. She wondered where she would get the courage to address the group.

She told a friend that she didn't think she would be able to speak. Then, he gave her advice that changed her life. "When you get before the group," he said, "talk to God and let them listen in."

A good person has good things in his heart. And so he speaks the good things that come from his heart. Matthew 12:35a (ICB)

That talk was one of the most inspiring Bonnie ever gave. The friend who counseled Bonnie, we might say, "was made for such a time as this."

Fast forward thirty years. Bonnie had been trying for three days to get her nails done. Finally, she decided to just go to a salon and take the first manicurist available. She took her seat and noticed another woman getting up from her chair and moving to another.

After about a minute, the woman got up and moved to a seat next to Bonnie.

"The first location was too cool," she said. "The second was actually colder. I think this one might be just right."

After they chatted for a while, the woman, Laura, mentioned that she had been preparing to be a counselor at her church but was now terrified at the prospect of actually speaking to someone.

Bonnie suggested, "Talk to God and let them listen in."

The woman broke out in tears. "This isn't me; I'm not a crier. But what you said touched my heart. I'll never forget it"

"You must have been sent by God," the manicurist whispered to Bonnie.

Bonnie gave Laura one of the hand-held crosses. She then gave her a second cross. "You'll know who to give this to."

"I know just who needs this," Laura said.

There is more! About a week later, Bonnie received the following text:

"Good morning Bon,

This is Laura I just wanted to let you know that I finally saw my friend last night and I gave her the cross that you gave me for her she immediately started crying and told me that when her husband was in the hospital that he used to pray with that exact same type of cross every day and somehow it got lost at the hospital when he passed away she was so grateful for it." ♥♥♥♥♥🙏🙏🙏🙏🙏

Sometimes it seems as if God micromanages our lives. Each of the individuals in this story had to be in just the right place at just the right time. Perhaps they were "made for such a time as this."

"Life is made up of moments. Perhaps this is the moment for which you have been created."—Quotation from a letter Bonnie received from her father.

BE A STAR THROWER

Poet Loren Eiseley wrote a beautiful essay titled "The Star Thrower," published in *The Unexpected Universe* (1969). I'd like to share with you another way to look at this story.

Once upon a time, there was a man who used to go to the ocean to do his writing. He had the habit of walking along the beach before he began his work. One day he was walking along the shore. As he looked down the beach, he saw a human figure moving like a dancer. He smiled to himself to think of someone who would dance on the beach, so he began to walk faster to catch up.

As he got closer, he saw that it was a young man, and the young man wasn't dancing; instead, he was reaching down, picking up something, and very gently throwing it into the ocean.

When he got closer, he called out, "Good morning! What are you doing?"

The young man paused, looked up and replied, "Throwing starfish into the ocean."

"I guess I should have asked, why are you throwing starfish into the ocean?"

"The sun is up and the tide is going out. If I don't throw them back, they'll die."

"But young man, don't you realize that there are miles and miles of beach covered with starfish? You can't possibly make a difference!"

The young man listened politely, then bent down, picked up another starfish, and threw it into the sea past the breaking waves. "It made a difference for that one."

This week we are looking at the starfishes in our lives: the people for whom we can make a difference. How can we make a difference? We can start by being an example. There is an old saying, "What you do speaks so much louder than what you say." As Christians, we serve as walking billboards for Jesus. People listen to what we say, watch what we do, and make judgments about the Gospel based on what they see in us.

You may be familiar with the story about the policeman who pulled a woman over after observing her making some rude gestures to another driver. The policeman demanded that she step out of the car, lean against the trunk, and keep her hands in sight at all times.

"But officer," she protested, "what did I do?"

"I suspect you are driving a stolen car," the policeman replied.

"But this is my car," she insisted, "What makes you think it is stolen?"

"Well," the officer explained, "I saw the 'I love Jesus' bumper sticker, and the 'John 3:16' window decal, then I saw your rude reaction to that other driver. Either the car is stolen, or somebody's been decorating it when you weren't looking."

Being a "Star-Thrower for Jesus is not just what we do on Sunday; it involves day-by-day, minute-by-minute decisions to watch what we say and do.

In the fifth chapter of Matthew, Verse 16, we read, *In the same way, let your good deeds shine out for all to see, so that everyone will praise your heavenly Father. Matthew 5:16 (NLT)*

Being kind and loving to others is a start, but our responsibility goes beyond just living a Christian life. Jesus commands us, *Go into all the world and preach the Good News to everyone. Mark 16:15b*

Going back to the story of the starfish, imagine that instead of a beach covered with threatened starfish, you see your neighborhood full of people facing a spiritual crisis. The Bible tells us, *Just as people are destined to die once, and after that to face judgment, so Christ was sacrificed once to take away the sins of many; and he will appear a second time, not to bear sin, but to bring salvation to those who are waiting for him. Hebrews 9:27-28 (NIV)*

Like the Star Thrower, we can make a difference. Mankind is struggling on this beach we call life. We can just pass by, or we can take advantage of every opportunity we have to offer hope. We share God's love when we share the Good News of Jesus.

We can invite others to go to church or welcome them into a small group or bible study. We can pass along a "Daily Word" magazine, or if we are moved by the Holy Spirit, we might even share our personal testimony. We can't save everyone, but we can make a difference by pointing some toward the One who can save them: Jesus, the original Star Thrower.

For I am not ashamed of the gospel, because it is the power of God that brings salvation to everyone who believes. Romans 1:16a

"All Week Long"

I won't be a Sunday Christian
whose week is filled with strife.
I'll do my best to pass the test
and show Christ in my life.
I'll wear a smile instead of a frown.
I'll spread encouragement all around.
I'll strive to share the joy I've found.
I'll be a Christian all week long.

I plan to be a mender,
a Band-Aid® for men's souls,
not a great pretender,
whose story's full of holes.
I plan to be a servant,
whose service shows God's heart,
a seed of hope for those I meet
who don't know where to start

I want to be like Jesus;
that "me" is years away.
Step by step, I'll get there;
Christ said, "He'll show the way."
I'll wear a smile instead of a frown.
I'll spread encouragement all around.
I'll choose to share the joy I've found.
I'll be a Christian all week long.

I urge you to live a life worthy of the calling you have received.

EPHESIANS 4:1B (NIV)

SHARING IN ACTION

MOMENT-BY-MOMENT

Only two check-out lines were open at Hobby Lobby (the Christian arts & crafts megastore). One line was dedicated to returns, and the line we were in had grown to about eight patrons. Suddenly, the clerk working our line placed a "Closed" sign on the counter which triggered immediate protests from the customers who were being sent to other terminals.

It took only a few seconds for the quiet mumbling to become a bit boisterous. We weren't happy about the inconvenience, but after commenting to each other about how the situation could have been handled better, we moved with the others to one of the working registers. Some of the other patrons weren't as compliant and the complaints started to get louder.

Out of the blue, Bonnie said loudly enough for everyone to hear, "This would be a great time to practice our Christianity!" The place became eerily quiet. Several people turned to smile at her, and even the most boisterous of the patrons, a young man who looked as if he might be in a motorcycle gang, quieted down. "Whew!" I thought. "That could have gotten really ugly. Praise God, it didn't."

Later, when Bonnie and I discussed the incident, she explained her boldness, "At church, we have been studying ways to live out our Christianity. What happened at Hobby Lobby is another example of sharing God's love. Sharing God's love involves striving with the best of our abilities to live Moment-by-Moment in ways that bring glory to God. Jesus' words come to mind: *In the same way, let your light shine before others, that they may see your good deeds and glorify your Father in heaven.* Matthew 5:16 (NIV)

If we take the sharing approach, we will discover a multitude of ways we can let our light shine. Every encounter with another person becomes an opportunity to do, say, or think something that glorifies God.

We aren't all equipped to fulfill the challenge Jesus spoke to his disciples: *"Therefore go and make disciples of all nations"* Matthew

28:19a (NIV). However each of us can, as we go into the world, offer a calming word, a loving gesture, or a shared prayer to demonstrate the difference the gospel has made in our lives.

In his letter to Titus, the apostle Paul offered advice every believer can take as a marching order: *In everything set them an example by doing what is good.* Titus 2:7a

ARE YOU AN EVANGELIST?

Recently, we were at Kaiser Hospital for a follow-up visit with my doctor. Bonnie was waiting in one of the nurse's cubicles for the results from a test when she noticed a cross and a few other decorations that indicate the person assigned to the cubicle is a Christian. When the male nurse who had been assisting me flashed Bonnie a "thumbs up," she asked him if the cubicle she was in was his.

"No! It belongs to someone else."

"Are you a Christian?" she asked.

"My mother is, and my brother and sister are."

"Allow me to suggest something," she said. "Mother's Day is Sunday. Take your mother to church. She will love it."

The nurse responded, "She would like that."

After I came out of the exam room and we started down the hall, Bonnie turned back toward the nurse and whispered, "She really would love it."

As we walked to the car she asked, "Is that evangelism? I don't do evangelism!"

Bonnie may not believe she has the gift of evangelism, but she, like all Christians, is called to spread the good news. *And then he told them, "Go into all the world and preach the Good News to everyone."* Mark 16:15 (NLT)

Normally, when people think of evangelism the first thing that comes to mind is the great evangelists: Dwight L. Moody, Billy Sunday, Billy Graham, T.D. Jakes, Greg Lorrie, Franklin Graham, Beth Moore, Rick Warren, and others. These powerful evangelists have had the spotlight, but millions of ordinary Christians also spread the Good News in their day-to-day interactions with others.

Evangelism can be defined as the spreading of the Good News of Jesus Christ by public preaching or personal witness (Adapted from the Oxford Dictionary). Let's focus on the personal witness approach.

Looking back at Bonnie's exchange with the nurse, we see three examples of spreading the Good News. First, there was the evangelism of the nurse who decorated her station. Next, we have Bonnie's words to the male nurse. Then, we have the potential conversation the young man could have with his mother and others about the "annoying lady" he met at the hospital.

St. Francis of Assisi purportedly said, "Preach the Gospel, and if necessary, use words." Anything we do that sheds light on the Good News of Jesus Christ is evangelism.

You are the light of the world. A town built on a hill cannot be hidden. Neither do people light a lamp and put it under a bowl. Instead they put it on its stand, and it gives light to everyone in the house. In the same way, let your light shine before others, that they may see your good deeds and glorify your Father in heaven. Matthew 5:14-16 (NIV)

Sometimes we can get so caught up in the things of this world that we lose sight of the world to come. In the book, *Seeing the Unseen: A Daily Dose of Eternal Perspective*, Randy Alcorn wrote, "For Christians, this present life is the closest they will come to Hell. For unbelievers, it is the closest they will come to Heaven . . .We can and should live with the perspective that will be ours one minute after we die."

With such an amazing story to tell . . .. We can all be evangelists.

How beautiful is the person who comes over the mountains to bring good news. How beautiful is the one who announces peace. He brings good news and announces salvation.

ISAIAH 52:7A (ICB)

TECHNO-GEEK EVANGELISM

The writers of the New Testament used epistles, handwritten letters delivered by a messenger, to share their faith and spread the Gospel. Today, "snail mail" has largely been replaced by email, posting on websites such as Instagram, LinkedIn, and Facebook, and with "tweets".

Which leads me to the topic of Twitter. As most of you know, Twitter is a social media network that has millions of users. Prior to 2017, when the rules changed, Twitter users were forced to get their point across in 140 characters or less. In some ways, Twitter's original approach reflected both scriptural and philosophical advice:

A truly wise person uses few words; a person with understanding is even-tempered. Proverbs 17:27 (NLT)

When there are many words, transgression and offense are unavoidable, but he who controls his lips and keeps thoughtful silence is wise. Proverbs 10:19 (AMP)

"If it takes a lot of words to say what you have in mind, give it more thought." – Dennis Roth

Brevity can be wonderful, but brevity can also be the enemy of understanding. Some things are just too important for the Twitter approach. Marriage proposals, breaking up a relationship and terminating an employee are best handled "face-to-face," using as many words as necessary (I've heard of all of these happening over social media).

Sharing your faith with friends and loved ones is another thing that is more appropriately handled face-to-face. Of course, we can't always have a face-to-face conversation. Friends and loved ones may live too far away. Some may feel uncomfortable and change the subject when you bring up the topic of faith. Then, there are millennials who may feel more comfortable "face-to-screen" than they are "face-to-face."

In a digital world, you may have to become a "Techno Geek" to get your message across. Where do you begin? Even something as simple as sharing a favorite Scripture may make a difference in someone's life. Adding a verse of Scripture below your signature on an email is one way to spread the Good News.

If you are on Facebook or LinkedIn, you can include a short testimony in the "Describe who you are" section. If you are compelled to use Twitter, share a verse or two, or even a short testimonial. One of the best ways to share the Gospel is to share your personal story. "Dear [contact name], I'd love to share with you the difference my faith has made in my life. "

When you share your personal story using social media, you may be blessed to interact with other Christians who welcome your message. Unfortunately, you may also encounter people who are disinterested, intolerant, or even hostile. The good news is that, up to this point in America, the greatest risk to "Techno Evangelism" is that someone will mark our emails as "spam," send us a nasty tweet, or, horror of horrors, "unfriend us."

> *For I am not ashamed of the gospel, because it is the power*
> *of God that brings salvation to everyone who believes: first*
> *to the Jew, then to the Gentile.*
>
> ROMANS 1:16 (NIV)

BLESSINGS ARE CONTAGIOUS

Dear children, let's not merely say that we love each other;
let us show the truth by our actions.
1 John 3:18 (NLT)

Bonnie was standing in line at a Family Christian Book Store behind a seven-year-old girl who was proudly holding a bright green bible with big pink flowers. "I'll bet you are getting your Bible engraved with pink letters," Bonnie said. The girl smiled brightly and moved toward the checkout where a young man was assisting customers.

Bon was purchasing a number of items, so she started searching in her purse for a coupon. Not finding one, she decided to just pay full price, since most of the proceeds go to charity anyway.

"I noticed you were looking for a coupon; I have an extra," the little girls' mother said.

"Thanks! That will be great. May I treat your daughter to her new Bible?"

"That OK. A hug and a thank-you is plenty."

As they hugged, the young man behind the counter exclaimed with laughter, "I wish we could get a video of this - two people trying to "out-bless" each other. The world needs to see more of this."

In the book *Charging the Human Battery* by Mac Anderson, we read, "And then some . . . These three little words are the secret to success. They are the difference between average people and top people in most companies. The top people always do what is expected . . . and then some. They are thoughtful of others; they are considerate and kind . . . and then some. They meet their responsibilities fairly and squarely . . . and then some. They are good friends and helpful neighbors . . . and then some. They can be counted on in an emergency . . . and then some. I am thankful for people like this, for they make the world a better place. Their spirit of service is summed up in these three little words . . . And then some."

Dear Heavenly Father, blessings are contagious. Help me to be a carrier of your love, doing what you'd expect . . . and then some.

SHOW YOUR THANKFULNESS

1st Thessalonians 5:16-18 (NIV) reminds us: *Rejoice always, pray continually, give thanks in all circumstances; for this is God's will for you in Christ Jesus.*

With this verse in mind, let's look at grace said at mealtime.

Jesus made it a habit to offer thanks before meals

And he directed the people to sit down on the grass. Taking the five loaves and the two fish and looking up to heaven, he gave thanks and broke the loaves. Then he gave them to the disciples, and the disciples gave them to the people. Matthew 14:19

Even when he was preparing for the Passion, Jesus gave thanks. *While they were eating, Jesus took bread, and when he had given thanks, he broke it and gave it to his disciples, saying, "Take and eat; this is my body."* Matthew 26:26

Grace is a prayer

Whether we offer a simple, "Praise God from whom all blessings flow," or take time to thank God for everyone from the farmer who planted the seed to the men from Waste Management who pick up the garbage, we offer grace for the blessings we have received.

Those who come from an Episcopalian background may be familiar with the prayer: Bless, O Lord, this food to our use and us to thy service, and make us ever mindful of the needs of others – In Jesus' name we pray, AMEN.

This prayer reminds us to be "mindful" of the needs of others. The Peace Center at Saddleback, South County Outreach, and food banks around the nation serve their communities by providing food for those less fortunate. Our donations of groceries can be tangible prayers of thanksgiving.

Grace is a way to witness

My niece decided to have her wedding reception at a buffet in Las Vegas. The sound of slot machines and people talking didn't provide the most romantic setting. But the atmosphere changed dramatically when she asked my brother to offer a prayer before the meal. You could have heard a pin drop. It seemed as if everyone stopped what they were doing and listened respectfully. When we pray in public, we become witnesses to the goodness of God. *"Give thanks to the Lord, for he is good. His love endures forever."* Psalm 136:1

In business situations or in groups that include people of different faiths, we may be uncertain what to do. We can show our love for God and our respect for others by asking those present if they would like to join us in a prayer of thanksgiving. If anyone present feels uncomfortable praying with us, we can simply bow our heads and offer a silent prayer.

There is a wonderful story in Acts 27 about the apostle Paul being on a ship caught in a hurricane. For fourteen days, the crew did what they could to save the ship. Just before dawn on the fifteenth day, Paul encouraged the men to eat. (Notice what he did next): *After he said this, he took some bread and gave thanks to God in front of them all. Then he broke it and began to eat.* Acts 27:35

The apostle Paul really meant it when he wrote, *Give thanks in all circumstances.*

Grace can take many forms:

Traditional
God is great! God is good!
Let us thank Him for our food. Amen.

Poetic
Thank you for the world so sweet.
Thank you for the food we eat.
Thank you for the birds that sing,
Thank you God for everything.
Author Unknown

Catholic
Bless us, oh Lord, and these thy gifts which we are about to receive from thy bounty, through Christ, our Lord. Amen.

Benedictus Benedicat (May the Blessed One bless)

Whether you are eating in the solitude of your home or sitting at the table of honor at a banquet, you have an opportunity to honor God with your prayer of thanksgiving. Remember, Thanksgiving is just a day; giving thanks is a lifestyle.

Give thanks to the Lord and proclaim his greatness. Let the whole world know what he has done.

1 CHRONICLES 16:8 (NLT)

THE MISSING PIECE

Do you have times when you feel like something is missing from your life? Maybe it's better health or wealth, or something or someone you think will make you feel complete—a missing piece that stands between you and a heart at peace.

Speaking in John 14:27a (NIV), Jesus said, *"Peace I leave with you; my peace I give you. I do not give to you as the world gives. Do not let your hearts be troubled and do not be afraid."* Jesus was telling his disciples that he offers a blessing that goes far beyond anything the world can offer.

How do we make the peace Jesus offers an essential piece in this puzzle we call life? Try as we might, there are times when it's hard to follow the Apostle Paul's advice as paraphrased in the Message Bible:

Don't fret or worry. Instead of worrying, pray. Let petitions and praises shape your worries into prayers, letting God know your concerns. Before you know it, a sense of God's wholeness, everything coming together for good, will come and settle you down. It's wonderful what happens when Christ displaces worry at the center of your life. Philippians 4:6-7 (MSG)

Life happens, and when petitions and praises don't yield the outcome desired, we need more than platitudes. Sometimes we can find our peace by offering comfort to someone who believes that their world is in pieces.

Often, the best way to comfort others is to just listen. If we must speak, we can speak to God and let others listen in, as we offer our prayers for them. We may not be able to supply the piece missing from their life, but with God's help, we can encourage them by sharing the peace we have known in the Lord.

"The deepest level of worship is praising God despite the pain, thanking God during the trials, trusting Him when we are tempted to lose hope, and loving Him when he seems so distant and far away. At my lowest, God is my hope. At my darkest, God is my light. At my weakest, God is my strength. At my saddest, God is my comforter." – Author unknown

> *All praise to God, the Father of our Lord Jesus Christ. God is our merciful Father and the source of all comfort. He comforts us in all our troubles so that we can comfort others. When they are troubled, we will be able to give them the same comfort God has given us.*

2 CORINTHIANS 1:3-4 (NLT)

COMFORTING THE GRIEVING

The Lord called home Joyce, a dear Christian friend. Heaven's gain is our loss. As we met with her husband of 63 years, we asked God to give us words that would comfort and strengthen him in this difficult time. Which brings us to the question, "How do you offer God's love to someone who has lost a loved one?"

Reflecting on the times that God has comforted you in times of trouble can bolster your faith and prepare your heart. *When doubts filled my mind, your comfort gave me renewed hope and cheer.* Psalm 94:19

In the third chapter of Ecclesiastes, we are reminded:

> *There is a right time for everything.*
> *Everything on earth has its special season.*
> *There is a time to be born*
> *and a time to die.*
> Ecclesiastes 3:1-2 (ICB)

> *There is a time to cry*
> *and a time to laugh.*
> *There is a time to be sad*
> *and a time to dance.*
> *There is a time to hug*
> *and a time not to hug.*
> Ecclesiastes 3:4-5

In those initial hours, expect tears—theirs and yours. Even Jesus wept for the friends and family of Lazarus. The person who is mourning may wonder if they ever again will feel like laughing or dancing, or even embracing.

While we know and believe the words of Romans 8:28 (NIV): *And we know that in all things God works for the good of those who love him, who have been called according to his purpose;* we also know that that in that initial season of mourning it's really difficult to see the good.

In Proverbs 20:12 we read, *"Ears that hear and eyes that see–The Lord has made them both."* God gave us two eyes that can help us see someone's pain and two ears that allow us to hear their story. Everyone expresses grief differently. For some, just listening to their stories is a good way to offer comfort. For others, sharing stories from our experiences can help them begin the healing process.

When it comes to prayer, asking, "Would you like me to pray with you?" is far more comforting and powerful than merely saying, "I will pray for you." *"For where two or three gather in my name, there am I with them."* Matthew 18:20

Sometimes it helps to share the reason for our hope with those who mourn. The Scriptures are replete with verses that talk about the hope we have in Christ. *Blessed are those who mourn, for they will be comforted.* Matthew 5:4

"For God so loved the world that he gave his one and only Son, that whoever believes in him shall not perish but have eternal life." John 3:16

Jesus said to her, "I am the resurrection and the life. The one who believes in me will live, even though they die," John 11:25

For we know that if the earthly tent we live in is destroyed, we have a building from God, an eternal house in heaven, not built by human hands. 2 Corinthians 5:1

But our citizenship is in heaven. And we eagerly await a Savior from there, the Lord Jesus Christ. Philippians 3:20

Therefore, holy brothers and sisters, who share in the heavenly calling, fix your thoughts on Jesus, whom we acknowledge as our apostle and high priest. Hebrews 3:1

'He will wipe every tear from their eyes. There will be no more death or mourning or crying or pain, for the old order of things has passed away." Revelation 21:4

What should Christians do or say when the person who has died did not know the Lord or when the one who mourns is a nonbeliever? At the memorial service for my late wife Jeannie, the pastor offered what could best be described as a "Hell-fire-and-damnation" sermon in place of a eulogy. Many of those in attendance were of differing faiths or had no faith. Several of the attendees mentioned to me how offended they felt.

That pastor would argue that as Christians the most loving thing we can do is share the Gospel. I'm not sure if anyone walked away from that service wanting to know much more about Jesus.

Keep this Scripture in mind: *But in your hearts revere Christ as Lord. Always be prepared to give an answer to everyone who asks you to give the reason for the hope that you have. But do this with gentleness and respect.* 1 Peter 3:15

You may find that the Proverbs 16:24 approach is a more effective way to share your faith.

> *"Kind words are like honey–sweet to the soul and healthy for the body."*
>
> PROVERBS 16:24 (NLT)

THE PRIVILEGE OF SERVING

WHATEVER YOU DO, WORK AT IT WITH ALL YOUR HEART,
AS WORKING FOR THE LORD, NOT FOR HUMAN MASTERS.

Colossians 3:23 (NIV)

IMPROVING YOUR SERVE

As a young man, I was an avid tennis player who had all the right equipment, all the right clothing, and a library of books full of tips on how to be a better player. One day I was walking through a bookstore when I spotted the book *Improving Your Serve*. My serve was already pretty good, but if the author Charles R. Swindoll had some tips, why not give them a try?

I bought the book without reading the sub-title, "The Art of Unselfish Living." The first chapter was "Who, Me a Servant?"

You've gotta be kidding, I thought. That book hit me right where it hurts. It made me realize I had been spending much more time practicing my tennis serve than I had ever spent practicing my Christianity by serving others.

Each of you should use whatever gift you have received to serve others, as faithful stewards of God's grace in its various forms. 1 Peter 4:10 (NIV)

It turned out, I was much more gifted as a servant than I had ever been as a tennis player. I didn't give up the sport; I just discovered a new love. Like Peter, who had denied Christ, I heard the words, "*Feed my sheep,*" and found myself working at a food bank. It was a blast! I was blessed far more than the people we served.

As Bonnie and I have moved into new areas of service, we try to follow the words in Ephesians: *Serve wholeheartedly, as if you were serving the Lord, not people, because you know that the Lord will reward each one for whatever good they do.* Ephesians 6:7-8a

E.B. White, the author of *Charlotte's Web*, wrote, "I arise in the morning torn between a desire to improve the world and a desire to enjoy the world." Why not both?

We have different gifts, according to the grace given to each of us. If your gift is prophesying, then prophesy in accordance with your faith; if it is serving, then serve; if it is teaching, then teach; if it is to encourage, then give encouragement; if it is giving, then give generously; if it is to lead, do it diligently; if it is to show mercy, do it cheerfully. Romans 12:6-8

Had I not found Chuck Swindoll's book, I might never have discovered the joy that comes from sharing God's love by serving others. In tennis, "love" means zero. In Christ, love is everything.

LET YOUR LIGHT SHINE

We don't get to play golf together often, so one afternoon Bonnie and I jumped at the chance to play. The pace of play was slow, so the sun was setting as we teed off on the fourteenth hole. By the time we reached the seventeenth hole, we could hardly see the green. "Let's play until we lose a ball," I suggested.

By the sound of her tee shot, I knew Bonnie had made good contact and the ball would be somewhere near the green. My ball ended up near hers and we had easy chips to the green. The problem was we could hardly see the green. Bonnie pulled out her cell phone and activated the flashlight, which I placed against the flag. Our light in the darkness allowed us to finish the hole.

"Better to light one little cell phone than to curse the darkness!"

There must be a lesson in there somewhere.

". . . and if you spend yourselves in behalf of the hungry and satisfy the needs of the oppressed, then your light will rise in the darkness, and your night will become like the noonday. The Lord will guide you always; he will satisfy your needs in a sun-scorched land and will strengthen your frame. You will be like a well-watered garden, like a spring whose waters never fail." Isaiah 58:10-11 (NIV)

"Like Well-Watered Gardens"

Trust God; He will guide you and strengthen your frame.
A spring never-ending, find joy in His name.
His light cuts through darkness to bless the oppressed.
Like well-watered gardens, by God, we are blessed.
Like well-watered gardens, when we kneel to pray,
The Lord sends his Spirit to show us the way
to love and redemption, set free from sin's stain,
our hearts become gardens when we let God reign.
So, we'll feed the hungry and give to the poor,
comfort the broken who come to our door.
Filled with God's Spirit, His light from above,
Our goal will be service, inspired by love.
Like well-watered gardens with paths that are clear,
Our lives can bear witness that Jesus is near.
By loving our neighbors and doing what's right,
like beautiful gardens, we'll grow in God's light.

This light of mine, I will let it shine . . . at home . . . in church . . . in my neighborhood . . . even on the golf course.

In the same way, let your light shine before others, that they
may see your good deeds and glorify your Father in heaven.

MATTHEW 5:16 (NIV)

IS IT WRONG TO FEEL GOOD ABOUT DOING GOOD

Is it wrong to feel good about doing good? This may seem like a silly question, but it can be a real conundrum for Christians who are concerned about becoming prideful. No wonder. The word "pride" appears in 63 verses in the New International Version of the Bible, most with a negative connotation. Here are just a few:

In his pride the wicked man does not seek him; in all his thoughts there is no room for God. Psalm 10:4 (NIV)

Let their lying lips be silenced, for with pride and contempt they speak arrogantly against the righteous. Psalm 31:18

Pride goes before destruction, a haughty spirit before a fall. Proverb 16:18

Yet, when we get to the book of Romans, we find the apostle Paul writing, *I am talking to you Gentiles. Inasmuch as I am the apostle to the Gentiles, I take pride in my ministry in the hope that I may somehow arouse my own people to envy and save some of them.* Romans 11:13-14

Notice that Paul took pride in his ministry. Where can satisfaction with a job well-done slip over into the destructive pride Scriptures warn against? A clue can be found in a definition found in Merriam Webster Dictionary: "PRIDE: the quality or state of being proud: such as inordinate self-esteem." Inordinate self-esteem might be further defined as ego run riot. As author Richard J. Hart explains, "EGO has a way of Edging God Out."

In Proverbs 16:18 pride is linked with "a haughty spirit." Turning again to our dictionary, haughty is defined as "blatantly and disdainfully proud: having or showing an attitude of superiority and contempt for people or things perceived to be inferior."

Don't think you are better than you really are. Be honest in your evaluation of yourselves, measuring yourselves by the faith God has given us. Just as our bodies have many parts and each part has a special function, so it is with Christ's body. We are many parts of one body, and we all belong to each other. Romans 12:3b-5 (NLT)

There are no small jobs when it comes to serving the Lord. The sexton who makes sure the doors of the church are unlocked is no less a servant of God than the evangelist who opens the doors of heaven to thousands. The apostle Paul offers guidance: *Pay careful attention to your own work, for then you will get the satisfaction of a job well done, and you won't need to compare yourself to anyone else.* Galatians 6:4

We started with the question, "Is it wrong to feel good about doing good?" Sometimes Christians miss out on the joy that comes from serving the Lord because they fear they will be condemned if they take any credit for the work they do. One wonderful man of God I know responds to any acknowledgment of his service with the words, "It's nothing. To God be the glory."

My friend's aim is to follow the directive: *If anyone speaks, they should do so as one who speaks the very words of God. If anyone serves, they should do so with the strength God provides, so that in all things God may be praised through Jesus Christ. To him be the glory and the power forever and ever. Amen.* 1 Peter 4:11 (NIV)

What my friend may be failing to appreciate is that there is a world of difference between saying, "Look at me; I did it." and saying, "I did it; *I can do all this through him who gives me strength.* Philippians 4:13 One appears ego-driven; the other is Spirit-driven.

My prayer is that this friend and many others could hear and appreciate the words the apostle Paul offered the Corinthians, *I have spoken to you with great frankness; I take great pride in you. I am greatly encouraged; in all our troubles my joy knows no bounds.* 2 Corinthians 7:4

Is it OK to take pride in what you do for the Lord? Satan would like nothing more than for you to "put your light under a basket." But feeling good about doing good and sharing your joy with others is another way, if done with humility, *to let your good deeds shine out for all to see, so that everyone will praise your heavenly Father.* Matthew 5:16b (NLT)

KOKO THE GORILLA

This story is dedicated to my co-author, my muse, my sweetheart, Bonnie Jane

Thirty-three plus years ago, Bonnie was a counselor at the Navy's Alcohol Rehabilitation Center (ARC) in Long Beach. Her job was to counsel members of the military who were compulsive overeaters, alcoholics, and other substance abusers.

Several months ago, Bonnie unexpectedly received a message from a former patient. He wrote, "I remember back at ARC, you told our group, "Seeing a picture of Koko the gorilla gently holding a kitten made you think of how you would feel wrapped in God's arms, fully protected, secure and loved.' I recalled that comparison when I read that Koko had died. Sad day. Koko was 46 years old."

Not everyone would draw a parallel between a gorilla gently holding a kitten and a loving God comforting one of His children, but Bonnie did. Just as each of us has a unique fingerprint, we all have our own ways of sensing what God is like. Your ideas may not comport 100% with what your neighbor thinks, and each of you may have your own understanding of Christian doctrine.

Sometimes we may be afraid to talk with others about our true beliefs. Even when we know the "theologically correct" response, we may be reluctant to ask questions for fear we will be put down. Some Christians, it seems, never heard that even when it comes to matters of faith, the only regrettable question is the one you don't ask.

The naive or inexperienced person [is easily misled and] believes every word he hears, But the prudent man [is discreet and astute and] considers well where he is going. Proverbs 14:15 (AMP)

When I have questions, I first go to the Scriptures and to Bible commentaries. If I don't find answers there, I seek out a brother or sister in Christ whom I trust, knowing they will be guided by the standard of 1st Timothy 3:15 (NIV):

But in your hearts revere Christ as Lord. Always be prepared to give an answer to everyone who asks you to give the reason for the hope that you have. But do this with gentleness and respect.

Occasionally, we may need the help of others to shore up our faith. Sometimes we can be a help to others. I once had a conversation with a woman who truly loves God and praises Jesus. She was troubled because she was having difficulty accepting the resurrection. I remember asking her, "Do you believe Jesus walked the Earth?"

"Yes, I do!" She replied emphatically.

"Do you believe that Jesus was crucified, died, and was buried?"

She said, "I saw the movie *The Case for Christ,* and I think the evidence is overwhelming, but I still have trouble with the resurrection."

"Where is Jesus right now?" I asked.

"I believe he is seated at the right hand of the Father."

"You don't doubt the resurrection," I offered. "You just don't understand the process. Me neither."

There may be some things we will only understand when we get to heaven. Got an unanswered question? God has an answer.

This is the confidence we have in approaching God: that if we ask anything according to his will, he hears us. 1 John 5:14

Bonnie feels the message she received from her former patient was the answer to one of her prayers. "I have been struggling with the question, does anything I do really make a difference? If something I shared thirty-three years ago is still having an impact in one man's life," she said with a tear in her eye, "maybe, I have been on the right path."

Show me your ways, Lord, teach me your paths.

PSALM 25:4

THE PRESIDENT IS CALLING

Imagine this: You are sitting having a nice cup of tea when the phone rings. You answer and are greeted by an official-sounding voice, "The President of the United States is calling." Moments later you hear the familiar voice of the President. He tells you he would like you to accept a position as a United States ambassador. You are shocked because nothing has prepared you for this prestigious assignment. "Please tell me more."

"As an ambassador, you will be my official voice. When you speak, it will be the same as if I myself were speaking. Your every action will be scrutinized—you will be the face of the United States to that country."

Now, it isn't likely our imagined scenario will ever occur, but as a Christian, you have already been given an even more important position. The apostle Paul explains it this way: *And God has given us this task of reconciling people to him. For God was in Christ, reconciling the world to himself, no longer counting people's sins against them. And he gave us this wonderful message of reconciliation.* 2 Corinthians 5:18b,19 (NLT)

Baker's Evangelical Dictionary explains reconciliation: "Reconciliation involves a change in the relationship between God and man or man and man. It assumes there has been a breakdown in the relationship, but now there has been a change from a state of enmity and fragmentation to one of harmony and fellowship."

When we share the Gospel of Jesus Christ, we are carrying a message of reconciliation. The wall that sin has erected between man and God has been torn down. We are ambassadors. So, *we are Christ's ambassadors; God is making his appeal through us. We speak for Christ when we plead, "Come back to God!* 2 Corinthians 5:20

It's fun to consider how we might feel if we received a call to become a United States ambassador. It's another thing altogether to consider the awesome responsibility we have as ambassadors for Christ. Speaking for the president might be difficult, but speaking for Christ . . . ?

*May the words of my mouth and the meditation of my heart
be pleasing to you, O Lord, my rock and my redeemer.*

PSALM 19:14

A PENCIL IN THE HAND

Have you ever received a hurtful letter that makes you stay up at night? It may have been sent by a friend or a family member. Maybe a business associate or someone whose political views are different from yours just had to let off steam, and they took it out on you. Regardless of the circumstances, the pain you felt was real, and you struggled with how to respond.

Sometimes these types of correspondence are based on misinformation. The person was told, or they perceived, that you had done or said something which you didn't. On occasion, regrettably, you may have done something offensive or damaging, and they had the right to address the issue, but the tone they took was unkind and, to put it bluntly, un-Christian.

Today, tweets and emails have replaced snail mail. Instant retaliation is too easy. Our first inclination may be to respond in kind, even though we know it's better to respond kindly. We need to ignore the devil on our shoulder and tune in to that angel who may be encouraging us to remember the words of the sometimes-hot-headed apostle, Peter:

Finally, all of you should be of one mind. Sympathize with each other. Love each other as brothers and sisters. Be tenderhearted, and .keep a humble attitude. Don't repay evil for evil. Don't retaliate with insults when people insult you. Instead, pay them back with a blessing. That is what God has called you to do, and he will grant you his blessing. 1 Peter 3:8-9 (NLT)

In Proverbs we read, *Don't ever stop being kind and truthful. Let kindness and truth show in all you do. Write them down in your mind as if on a tablet.* Proverbs 3:3 (ICB)

The apostle Paul was thinking about things we say and do when he wrote, *You show that you are a letter from Christ that he sent through us. This letter is not written with ink, but with the Spirit of the living God. It is not written on stone tablets. It is written on human hearts.* 2 Corinthians 3:3

Mother Teresa (Saint Teresa of Calcutta) echoed the thought, "I am like a pencil in the hand of a writing God who is sending a love letter to the world." We, too, are pencils in the hand of a writing God. We show our hearts by how we communicate with others. What do your communications say about your heart?

> *So may the words of my mouth, my meditation-thoughts, and every movement of my heart be always pure and pleasing, acceptable before your eyes, my only Redeemer, my Protector-God.*
>
> PSALM 19:14 (TPT)

FOCUSED ON LOVE OVER LOSS

It started about two years ago when Cindy, one of the women who attends the Saddleback chapel service we co-hosted with several other volunteers, was going through an especially difficult time. Bonnie and another volunteer, Ariel, would stop by her room each Saturday to pray with her.

"Then, we got the idea," Bonnie explained, "that it would be a great comfort to Cindy if we could get Pastor Rick to come and give her a hug. But with a worldwide ministry, Pastor Rick has such a hectic schedule, we were reluctant to ask him to visit our small congregation. Besides, the hug was our idea, not hers."

During a visit to a small church in Arkansas, Bonnie asked the congregation to pray for Cindy. After the service, she told one of the worship leaders, "I think that a hug from Rick would be a miracle for her."

The worship leader hugged Bonnie and said, "Maybe you are her miracle!"

It turned out that a hug from Pastor Rick would have been a momentary treat. God had bigger plans. When Cindy shared her personal testimony at one of the chapel services, Bonnie knew Cindy's was a story that had to be shared. Working with Cindy, we drafted the text that became the story "Focused on Love Over Loss." That story was included in the Saddleback bulletin that was distributed to tens of thousands of people worldwide.

Dream small and see what God has in store for you.

Many are the plans in a person's heart, but it is the LORD's purpose that prevails. Proverbs 19:21 (NIV)

Focused on Love over Loss
05/31/2018 – Don Sennott, Guest Storyteller

"I don't know why I'm here," Cindy said, referring to the automobile accident that almost took her life. "I should have died; it was a real bad accident."

Cindy recalls that her daughter, Kristen, was in the car with her when the accident happened. But Kristen was not injured as severely as her mom. Cindy tried to remember more details, but the words just wouldn't come. The head injuries from the accident were devastating, and Cindy now lives with limitations that very easily could have shaken her faith.

"I forget stuff," she continued. "I just don't remember much about the accident."

Everyday activities that many of us take for granted are serious challenges for Cindy. Caregivers assist her when she showers, help her braid her hair and check in on her at bedtime. At 55 years of age, Cindy is younger than most residents at her assisted-living facility.

"There is one guy younger than me, but that's it," Cindy said. "I'm not sure how long I've been here . . . a long time, but I like it more than the place I was before."

When asked what impact the accident had on her faith in God, Cindy smiled big and declared, "My faith got lifted up—got higher, higher, higher!" Then, Cindy said something that made it clear the Holy Spirit is truly at work in her life, "The love of God is bigger than my losses."

Every Saturday, a team of volunteers from Saddleback Church hosts a worship service for Cindy's assisted-living community. They offer prayers, share a video message, sing hymns, and give hugs and words of encouragement.

Recently, Bonnie, one of the Saddleback volunteers, was leading the discussion that followed a video message from Pastor Rick. "What does Jesus mean to you?" she asked. There was a moment of silence as the attendees pondered the question. Cindy leaned forward in her chair, hugged herself, and shouted enthusiastically, "I love Jesus so much. I love the Lord with all my heart, soul, and strength."

Cindy had no way of knowing how impactful her personal witness would be. She hadn't prepared a speech; she just spoke from her heart. Bonnie later shared, "I can't find the words to capture the power that was projected in her testimony. How could someone who has lost so much still love God this much?"

A big part of the answer is her involvement with Saddleback Church. Cindy remembers attending Saddleback when services were still being held in tents. One of Cindy's cherished possessions is a picture taken when Pastor Rick visited her at the assisted-living community after her accident. "Pastor Rick would pray for me. That made me feel good!" Cindy explained with a strong emphasis on the word "good." She hugged herself and said, "He's a big dude."

When asked what brought her to Christ, Cindy praised her mom and her sister. Holding back tears, she pointed skyward and added, "My Mom's on the other side of eternity now."

Saddleback continues to be a powerful presence in Cindy's life. Before the accident, her mother and sister would encourage her to attend. Now, volunteers in the Saddleback Assisted Living Ministry help her keep a strong connection with Jesus.

When asked how long she has been attending the Saddleback service in the chapel, Cindy replied, "I don't know . . . a long time. I love coming to chapel." She paused to think. "Rick Muchow used to come. He was good, too," she said. "I love to sing hymns. 'What a Friend We Have in Jesus' is one of my favorites."

"I love to worship Jesus," Cindy continued. "The Saddleback service gives me lots of hopes and lots of dreams. I hope Jesus will heal me, and I dream of seeing him in heaven." She smiles and adds, "I am grateful I can still be of service."

ARE YOU TOO OLD TO DREAM?

Gray hair is a crown of splendor; it is attained in the way of righteousness. Proverbs 16:31 (NIV)

After the chapel service, during which the topic had been "God's Dream for Your Life," one of the residents of the assisted living community approached Bonnie and me and asked, "Why do most sermons seem to be directed at young people?"

To many seniors, building dreams seems like yesterday's opportunity. "Who can dream," they may wonder, "when it is a major challenge to just push my walker to the dining room?"

> *The lofty plans I made as a youth seem silly in retrospect.*
> *The dreams I dreamed are dreams no more.*
> *What now? I must reflect.*
> *I know there still are mountains to climb*
> *And streams that I must ford.*
> *But I've grown old; my strength has waned;*
> *How can I serve the Lord?*

Is building dreams yesterday's opportunity? Do all the promises found in the Bible have a date code—use before age . . ., or can we still dream dreams? Was God speaking only to the exiles, or can God's words in Jeremiah offer us hope? *"For I know the plans I have for you," declares the Lord, "plans to prosper you and not to harm you, plans to give you hope and a future.* Jeremiah 29:11

A dear 94-year old lady, who recently went to be with the Lord, used to pull us close and ask, "Why am I still here—what is my purpose?" She would. sit in the chapel service softly singing the words to "Jesus Loves Me." Little did she know how often her simple song lifted our spirits. She had a dream to serve God, and it turned out she did serve Him to the very end.

Words from a poem by CT Studd come to mind:

> *Give me Father, a purpose deep,*
> *In joy or sorrow Thy word to keep;*
> *Faithful and true what e'er the strife,*
> *Pleasing Thee in my daily life;*
> *Only one life, 'twill soon be past,*
> *Only what's done for Christ will last.*

What is God's dream or His purpose for our lives? Perhaps we, like Timothy are called to be a coworker with Christ.

He is our beloved brother and coworker with God in preaching the gospel. We knew he would strengthen your faith and encourage your hearts so that no one would be shaken by these persecutions, for you know that we are destined for this. 1 Thessalonians 3:2-3 (TPT)

We can all dream of making a difference. The place to start is where we are. Maybe it's too late for us to, as Jesus commanded, "*As you go into all the world, preach openly the wonderful news of the gospel to the entire human race!* Mark 16:15 But so long as we are living, we have opportunities to share with those in our part of the world.

Chapter 12 of Romans is a guidebook on how we can achieve our dream of making a difference.

Don't copy the behavior and customs of this world, but let God transform you into a new person by changing the way you think. Then you will learn to know God's will for you, which is good and pleasing and perfect. Romans 12:2 (NLT)

Don't just pretend to love others. Really love them. Hate what is wrong. Hold tightly to what is good. Love each other with genuine affection, and take delight in honoring each other. Romans 12:9-10

Do all that you can to live in peace with everyone. Romans 12:18

When I was twenty-five, I bemoaned the fact I was a quarter of a century old. At fifty, I was shocked to realize I was half of a century old. As I approach seventy-five, it's finally sinking in: I am a newborn in terms of eternity.

"In the last days,' God says, I will pour out my Spirit upon all people. Your sons and daughters will prophesy. Your young men will see visions, and your old men will dream dreams."

ACTS 2:17

BUILDING RELATIONSHIPS

THEREFORE, WHENEVER WE HAVE THE OPPORTUNITY,
WE SHOULD DO GOOD TO EVERYONE—
ESPECIALLY TO THOSE IN THE FAMILY OF FAITH.

Galatians 6:10 (NLT)

THE COVENANT PRAYER

Love is patient, love is kind. It does not envy, it does not boast, it is not proud. It does not dishonor others, it is not self-seeking, it is not easily angered, it keeps no record of wrongs. Love does not delight in evil but rejoices with the truth. It always protects, always trusts, always hopes, always perseveres. 1 Corinthians 13:4-7 (NIV)

1st Corinthians 13 is frequently read at weddings, so no one was surprised when Anthony and Daven selected the above verses as part of their ceremony. However, many in the congregation were astonished when the friend they had chosen to read the verse inadvertently turned instead to Romans 13 and read the following:

For the one in authority is God's servant for your good. But if you do wrong, be afraid, for rulers do not bear the sword for no reason. They are God's servants, agents of wrath to bring punishment on the wrongdoer. Therefore, it is necessary to submit to the authorities, not only because of possible punishment but also as a matter of conscience.

This is also why you pay taxes, for the authorities are God's servants, who give their full time to governing. Give to everyone what you owe them: If you owe taxes, pay taxes; if revenue, then revenue; if respect, then respect; if honor, then honor. Romans 13:4-7

Daven and Anthony have been happily married for over twenty years, and as far as I know, neither has had any problems with the Internal Revenue Service. As for those that attended the wedding, they probably wouldn't have taken notice had the young friend read from 1st Corinthians, as planned. But few, if any, have forgotten the look on Daven's face as their friend read the unexpected verses from Romans.

Bonnie and I celebrate our anniversary on July 3rd. When people ask how we met, Bonnie often kiddingly tells them we met on eBay, to which I respond, "That's right. She was the only one who would bid!" In fact, we met on eHarmony.

Neither of us can claim we know all the secrets to a harmonious relationship. As with most marriages, we have good days and bad; Praise God . . . mostly good. We believe praying together at the start of each day has helped us keep things in perspective. Every morning since our wedding, whether together or speaking over the phone while away, we have taken time to renew the commitment we made to each other in our Covenant Prayer. We pray God will continue to be the third strand in the cord that holds us together.

Though one may be overpowered, two can defend themselves. A cord of three strands is not quickly broken. Ecclesiastes 4:12

We once heard a pastor explain that this verse describes a true covenant relationship. The "two" are the man and wife who are being joined in holy matrimony. The "third cord," the most important one, is God.

In our Covenant Prayer, we also pray, by name, for many of those who are part of our lives. It might seem like that would take all day, but normally it takes less than fifteen minutes.

For those who have lost a loved one, we encourage you to hold onto the good memories. Bonnie and I are widow/widower. We praise God every day for how God blessed us with our former mates, John Wyatt and Jeannie Sennott, who loved us, nurtured us, and helped prepare us for this phase of our lives.

This is our version of a Covenant Prayer:

> *Dear heavenly Father,*
>
> *Look with favor on the world you have made and for which your Son gave his life, and especially on Bonnie and me, as we celebrate the covenant, we have made with you and with each other.*
>
> *Give us wisdom and devotion each day that we may each be to the other a strength in need, a counselor in perplexity, a comfort in sorrow, and a companion in joy. Grant that our wills may be so knit together in your will and our spirits in your Spirit that we may grow in love and peace with you and one another all the days of our lives.*

Give us such fulfillment of our mutual affection that we may reach out in love and concern for others. Make our life together a sign of Christ's love, that unity may overcome loneliness, forgiveness heal guilt, and joy conquer despair.

Thank you for our children, our grandchildren, and our extended family. Keep them safe and protected in your care.

We ask you to protect our country and its leaders, the policemen, firemen, and military personnel who protect us. We are praying, believing it is your will to bless and protect our friends, our neighbors, and those we connect with as we walk through today.

We pray for those who don't yet know Jesus and the power of God's love.

We pray for the residents, the volunteers and the staff in hospitals, assisted living communities, homeless shelters, prisons, and other places where your children are cared for.

Lord, we thank you for all those, living and departed, who have helped us to become who we are. We ask you to help us forgive any who have hurt us and to forgive us for anyone we have hurt.

We praise you and thank you for all the blessings of this life and ask you to show us your will for us, and give us the power to carry it out this day and always. In Jesus' Name, we pray. AMEN

Adapted from the marriage prayer found in the Book of Common Prayer According to the use of the Episcopal Church

Besides our morning prayer, we have adopted another practice we think can help any couple reach that "happily ever after" we all desire. In those times when we get cranky, and we both have times we get cranky, we offer each other a "twenty-four-hour pass." This pass is our way of following another Scripture: *Always be humble and gentle. Be patient with each other, making allowance for each other's faults because of your love. Make every effort to keep yourselves united in the Spirit, binding yourselves together with peace.* Ephesians 4:2-3 (NLT)

We also have learned that there are 10 things about another person that will never change, so try to accept them. More about that in the next story.

Does this mean we live up to the standard set in 1st Corinthians 13? We try!

Does it mean we each strive to be as strong a strand as possible in the three-strand cord described in Ecclesiastes? Absolutely!

Bonnie and I frequently interact with couples who have been married forty, fifty, even sixty years. Those who seem the most content are the ones who have put the Lord at the center of their lives and who recognize that forgiveness is the oil that keeps marriages running smoothly.

"Satisfy us each morning with your unfailing love, so we may sing for joy to the end of our lives." Psalm 90:14

As we were working on this chapter, we learned that two people we love very much have decided to divorce. We pray God will guide each of them as they move forward. We also ask you to pray for them and for anyone you may know who has been separated from another by divorce or death.

TEN THINGS THAT WILL NEVER CHANGE

A few years ago, we heard the following words of wisdom, "In any relationship, there are ten things about the other person that will irritate you, and those things will never change." Oh! Those pesky ten things. Whether you're talking about your mate, a sibling, your child, a friend, or a business associate, given enough time, you will find there are ten things about the other person that will irritate you. And no matter how much you try to make that person change, they can't or won't!

Now, we aren't talking about addictions or major character defects like dishonesty or abusiveness; those require intervention and prayer. Rather, we are talking about those little quirks or habits that can really get under your skin.

Bonnie likes to tease that I have at least two dozen of those immutable irritants . . . and the number keeps growing. Take, for instance, my use of puns. If she had her way, I'd be put in a *punitentiary* . . ., see what I mean?

Since we all will have to deal with those "ten things," the question becomes, how can we prevent the ten things from damaging an otherwise wonderful relationship? A starting point is found in Reinhold Niebuhr's *Serenity Prayer.*

> *God grant me the serenity to*
> *accept the things I cannot change,*
> *the courage to change the things I can,*
> *and the wisdom to know the difference.*

Accepting "the things we cannot change" begins with accepting the fact they indeed cannot or will not change. Then, follow the wisdom found in Proverbs 21:9 (MSG), *Better to live alone in a tumbledown shack than share a mansion with a nagging spouse* (or sibling, or friend, etc.,) No one ever nagged or even loved someone else to perfection.

Having the courage to change the things we can change begins with changing the one thing we can control: our attitude. Jesus commanded us, "*Love each other.*" He didn't say, "Love each other except when . . ."

Having the wisdom to know the difference begins with prayer. *We continually ask God to fill you with the knowledge of his will through all the wisdom and understanding that the Spirit gives, so that you may live a life worthy of the Lord and please him in every way: bearing fruit in every good work, growing in the knowledge of God.* Colossians 1:9b-10 (NIV)

Since those ten or more things aren't going to change, learn to focus on the good things you pray will never change. *Accept one another, then, just as Christ accepted you, in order to bring praise to God.* Romans 15:7

THE FIRST FIFTEEN MINUTES

The first fifteen minutes may be the most important fifteen minutes of your day, especially if you use them to (1) Make your bed, (2) Pray, and (3) Read Scripture.

In the book, *Make Your Bed - Little Things That Can Change Your Life . . . And Maybe the World*, Admiral William H. McRaven shares lessons he learned going through Navy Seal Training and as a member of a Seal Combat team.

His first lesson: "*If you want to change the world . . .* start off by making your bed." Admiral McRaven explains, "Nothing can replace the strength and comfort of one's faith, but sometimes the simple act of making your bed can give you the lift you need to start your day and provide you the satisfaction to end it right."

Travel back in time to approximately 1010-970 B.C. and you'll encounter another warrior who demonstrated how to start your day off right. King David knew that the Lord listens to prayers, so he prayed every morning.

Lord, every morning you hear my voice. Every morning, I tell you what I need. And I wait for your answer. Psalm 5:3 (ICB)

Morning, noon, and night I cry out in my distress, and the Lord hears my voice. Psalm 55:17 (NLT)

David was bold in asking for the things he needed, but his humility was evident as he saturated his prayers with thanks and praise.

But as for me, I will sing about your power. Each morning I will sing with joy about your unfailing love. For you have been my refuge, a place of safety when I am in distress. Psalm 59:16

Enter his gates with thanksgiving; go into his courts with praise. Give thanks to him and praise his name. For the Lord is good. His unfailing love continues forever, and his faithfulness continues to each generation. Psalm 100:4-5

King David also added a period of meditation and instruction to his morning routine. In the Psalms, we see how much David depended on the Scriptures (for him, the Torah).

I rise early, before the sun is up; I cry out for help and put my hope in your words. Psalm 119:147

Lord, teach me what you want me to do. And I will live by your truth. Teach me to respect you completely. Psalm 86:11 (ICB)

Your word is a lamp for my feet, a light on my path. I have taken an oath and confirmed it, that I will follow your righteous laws. Psalm 119:105-106 (NIV)

The first fifteen minutes may indeed be the most important fifteen minutes of your day. When you make your bed, you start the day with an accomplishment. When you pray, you make a connection with God that can strengthen and comfort you in the tougher minutes of the day, and when you take time to read a few verses of Scripture, you come closer to learning God's purpose for your life.

If you want to change the world, a good place to start is in your own bedroom. Make your bed, Pray, and read from God's Word. Then, share God's love with all you meet.

Always be happy. Never stop praying. Give thanks whatever happens. That is what God wants for you in Christ Jesus.

1 THESSALONIANS 5:16-18 (ICB)

KISSES IN HIS POCKET

Bonnie shared with me how she used to say, "kisses in your pocket" before sending her daughter Dawn off to school. Her story reminded me of the many things my Mom did for me, such as sending me off to school with candy to make my day a little sweeter. This poem is offered as a tribute to mothers everywhere.

Maybe there is someone in your life who needs a "kiss" from you today.

"Kisses in his Pocket"

She placed kisses in his pocket and sent him on his way,
reminders of his Mother's love that helped him through the day.
Whenever he felt lonely, whenever he felt sad,
he'd hold her kiss up to his lips, and things just weren't as bad.
Those precious pocket kisses are memories he can hold.
So dear, and yet so far away, the child has grown old.
And though the Mom that put them there is with the Lord above,
he still can taste a chocolate kiss and thank God for her love.

I will comfort you as a mother comforts her child.

ISAIAH 66:13A (ICB)

FATHERS USED TO BE HEROES

Fathers used to be heroes in television shows. *Father Knows Best, The Danny Thomas Show, Leave It to Beaver,* and *The Rifleman* all featured strong father figures.

In 1971, Archie Bunker, the bigoted patriarch of the Bunker family, became the new model for TV dads. *Everybody Loves Raymond* followed, with Peter Boyle playing the disheveled spouse of the cantankerous Marie. Nowadays, if you want to see how fathers are presented on television, you must turn to offerings such as *Modern Family, Family Guy,* and *The Simpsons.*

"Honor your father and your mother, as the Lord your God has commanded you, so that you may live long and that it may go well with you in the land the Lord your God is giving you." Deuteronomy 5:16 (NIV)

Based on the way fathers are presented in today's TV shows, I think it's safe to say, "Deuteronomy was not required reading in the Theater Arts Department."

It's no secret; fathers don't always know best. Fathers get some things right and some things wrong. Unfortunately, the things they get wrong often have the biggest impact on their families.

My father was a good partner for my Mom, raising two daughters and two sons. Like other dads, he saw home as a teapot where he could let off steam after a pressure-filled day. He could be demanding, impatient, and caustic when he spoke with my siblings and me.

Thankfully, he was always respectful when he spoke with our Mom. On the job and in public, my father was friendly, generous, kind, and—now that I think about it—gentle. His favorite Bible verse was, *My dear brothers and sisters, take note of this: Everyone should be quick to listen, slow to speak and slow to become angry.* James 1:19

Ed, as we sometimes called him when he wasn't listening, used to joke about our family name. The motto on our family crest read, "Aim High; Speak Low; Fear God, and Sin Not."

"We had to change the name from Sinnot to Sennott," he would say. "We just couldn't live up to the *'sin not'* part!" He teased about it, but my father tried to live a life worthy of his calling. He loved the Lord, valued integrity, and did his best to follow the wisdom of Proverbs: *Start children off on the way they should go, and even when they are old they will not turn from it.* Proverbs 22:6

It took me a long time to appreciate just how good a man my father was. He'll be among the first people I want to speak with when I get to heaven.

It also took too many years for me to realize that many people, if not most, were not blessed to have a dad as good as mine. Those with fathers who were absent or abusive have spoken to me about how difficult it has been for them to move past childhood memories of a "bad" father and trust their heavenly Father to be a "good" Father. As the title of the Chris Tomlin song reminds us, God is not just a good Father; He is a "Good, Good Father."

It is a comfort to know we have a good, good heavenly Father who is still our hero.

See what great love the Father has lavished on us, that we should be called children of God! And that is what we are!

1 JOHN 3:1A

NO PERFECT PARENTS—NO PERFECT KIDS

Have you ever wondered what your parents would think of what you've made of your life? I do, and I know they would have both positive and negative opinions. I'm sure my Mom would concentrate on the good and overlook my many missteps. Many moms are like that.

My Dad would probably wonder where he could have done a better job of training me.

Train up a child in the way he should go: and when he is old, he will not depart from it. Proverbs 22:6 (KJV)

If I could speak with my folks, who have both passed on, I would let them know I believe they did the best they could. There are no perfect parents, and kids don't always turn out great either.

We see proof of this in some of our Bible heroes: Adam's son Cain was a hard worker, but he was jealous and murdered his brother. Lamech's son Noah was a great ark builder, but he drank too much. Isaac's son Jacob was the father of the twelve tribes of Israel, but with the assistance of his mother Rebekah, he conned his brother Esau out of his inheritance. Jacob raised sons who so hated their brother Joseph they sold him into slavery.

Manoah's son Samson became a great warrior, but his affair with Delilah led to his destruction. Jesse's son David was "a man after God's own heart." He was also an adulterer and an accomplice to murder. David's son Absalom took part in a rebellion against him, and his son Solomon (who, by the way, wrote Proverb 22) loved the Lord and built His temple, but . . . *As Solomon grew old, his wives turned his heart after other gods, and his heart was not fully devoted to the Lord his God, as the heart of David his father had been.* 1 Kings 11:4 (NIV)

I imagine every one of those Bible heroes had times when they wished they had done things differently. After I became a father, I was tempted to tear out the page of my NIV Bible that includes Ephesians 6:4: *Fathers, do not exasperate your children; instead, bring them up in the training and instruction of the Lord.* My boys can testify; I majored in exasperation!

Every parent would feel blessed if their children would heed Proverbs 1:8: *Listen, my son, to your father's instruction and do not forsake your mother's teaching.* Our instruction may not always be the best, and our teaching can fall on ears unwilling to listen. A friend wears a T-shirt with the message: "To Be Old and Wise, You Must First Be Young and Stupid."

There are no perfect parents, and there are no perfect children, but there are plenty of perfect moments along the way. – Dave Willis

If we keep in mind there are no perfect parents, no perfect kids, we can build families where Romans 12:18 becomes a guiding principle–*If it is possible, as far as it depends on you, live at peace with everyone.*

The Passion translation offers an expanded list of the qualities of love. It might be worth posting somewhere where all family members can read it.

> *Love is large and incredibly patient. Love is gentle and consistently kind to all. It refuses to be jealous when blessing comes to someone else. Love does not brag about one's achievements nor inflate its own importance. Love does not traffic in shame and disrespect, nor selfishly seek its own honor. Love is not easily irritated or quick to take offense. Love joyfully celebrates honesty and finds no delight in what is wrong. Love is a safe place of shelter, for it never stops believing the best for others. Love never takes failure as defeat, for it never gives up.*

1 Corinthians 13:4-7 (TPT)

When there is friction between family members, our challenge as Christians is to take the first step toward peace. Sadly, there are situations when the bond between family members has been broken. Sometimes the wounds are so deep, the walls of resentment so cemented with unforgiveness that peace is but a distant hope. This is when praying for the one who hurt you is the surest path to forgiveness and healing.

Do not be angry with each other, but forgive each other. If someone does wrong to you, then forgive him. Forgive each other because the Lord forgave you. Colossians 3:13 (ICB)

One of my friends had a tough time relating to his teenage son. He wanted to be a good father but felt he was failing. His need to maintain control was sending their relationship out of control. Many parents feel the same way.

Lord, help me repent. I must let him vent.
No matter my intent, he's spent and wonders where hope went.
He needs my ears, not my advice. A smile will suffice,
or a touch, not too much.
He'll be just fine. Solutions are yours, not mine.
Not my will but Thine.
Lord, please touch his soul by taking control.
I'm just his Dad. Today he needs his Father.

Over the years, I have seen a lot of "Father of the Year" mugs, "World's Best Mom" T-shirts, and "My Kid is Special" bumper stickers. Nice! But the bumper sticker I'd love to see is one that reads, "My Father in Heaven is Perfect. Top that!"

WHEN ELEPHANTS FIGHT

A group of men was discussing the impact parents have on the personalities of their children. A discussion question from the study guide they were using suggested that each give three words that would describe their parents. The words offered ran the gamut from loving, kind, and supportive to missing, neglectful, and abusive. Even those who had positive feelings about their parents admitted their parents had been far from perfect.

None of us is perfect. Yet, even good parents feel the burden of their imperfection. It seems ironic that Jesus' words, *"But you are to be perfect, even as your Father in heaven is perfect."* Matthew 5:48 (NLT) come at the end of a lesson on loving your enemies. In families, battle lines can be drawn; loved ones can become adversaries. Why the conflict? There are as many reasons as there are families, but one common problem is unrealistic expectations. Parents can expect too much of their children, and children, once they start to build their own identity, can expect too much of their parents.

One of the men in the group had been born in Nigeria. His birth father had passed away when he was two years old, and his mother had married his father's brother. He used a Nigerian proverb to explain the damage caused by the conflict between his mother and his stepfather. "When adult elephants fight," he said, "they are careful not to hurt the tender grass around them. The elephants," he explained, "are symbolic of adults, while the tender grass represents the children."

Parents forget, or more likely never learned, how fragile children can be. On the flip side, as children mature, they can forget how fragile their parents may be.

Try to think of three words to describe each person in your family. This exercise is a good way to come to a better understanding of your feelings about a mother/father/child/or sibling who may have left a negative imprint on you.

When I was asked, for example, what three words would describe my father, I had no problem listing intelligence, integrity, and impatience. As I thought about each word, I realized the positive and negative imprints my father had made on me and on my approach to parenting. For me, healing came when I took the time to ponder what had been the damaging impact of my father's impatience.

The first thing I realized was that the number of times he had been patient far outnumbered the times when he lost his patience. One "Aw shucks," as they say, will erase a hundred "atta-boys."

The second thing I realized was that I had often given him cause to be impatient (either accidentally or on purpose).

Friends have told me that a single incident or a handful of incidents clouded their appreciation of any good their parents may have done. Others have shared stories of experiences that were so abusive they don't know how to begin the process of healing. Sometimes, we need to allow the dust settle, then pray that God will guide us as we seek to give and receive the forgiveness that promotes family unity.

When you list the three words that best describe anyone who may have trampled your "emotional grass," I encourage you to have a heart that longs for reconciliation.

> Since God chose you to be the holy people he loves, you must clothe yourselves with tenderhearted mercy, kindness, humility, gentleness, and patience. Make allowance for each other's faults, and forgive anyone who offends you. Remember, the Lord forgave you, so you must forgive others. Above all, clothe yourselves with love, which binds us all together in perfect harmony.
>
> COLOSSIANS 3:12-14

SIBLING RIVALRY

Jesus replied: "'Love the Lord your God with all your heart and with all your soul and with all your mind.' This is the first and greatest commandment. And the second is like it: 'Love your neighbor as yourself.
Matthew 22:37-39 (NIV)

Love the Lord—Check!

Love your Neighbors—Check!

Love your brothers and sisters—Not mentioned!

Perhaps Jesus recognized that the family unit isn't always the best breeding ground for love. Take his own family for instance. Both Matthew and Mark tell us Jesus had four brothers and at least two sisters. His half-brother James eventually became the leader of the Church in Jerusalem. James and half-brother Jude wrote epistles. But there are hints in Jesus teaching that there may have been tension on the home front.

Jesus said to them, "A prophet is not without honor except in his own town, among his relatives and in his own home." Mark 6:4

Look at how Jesus responded when he was told his mother and brothers wished to speak with him:

While Jesus was still talking to the crowd, his mother and brothers stood outside, wanting to speak to him. Someone told him, "Your mother and brothers are standing outside, wanting to speak to you."

He replied to him, "Who is my mother, and who are my brothers?" Pointing to his disciples, he said, "Here are my mother and my brothers. For whoever does the will of my Father in heaven is my brother and sister and mother." Matthew 12:46-50

When Jesus spoke of anger, he targeted anger between brothers and sisters:

"But I tell you that anyone who is angry with a brother or sister will be subject to judgment. Again, anyone who says to a brother or sister, 'Raca' [an Aramaic term of contempt] is answerable to the court. And anyone who says, 'You fool!' will be in danger of the fire of hell." Matthew 5:22

The Old Testament is replete with stories about conflicts between siblings. Cain and Abel, Moses with his sister Miriam, Jacob and Esau, Joseph and his brothers, King David's sons Amnon and Absalom, and Jehoram who put his brothers to death . . . to name a few of the more extreme cases.

Today, sibling rivalry provides the plotline for many of our sitcoms and dramas. We laugh at sibling rivalry when we see it on the screen but are hurt and angered when it becomes part of our life.

I was the youngest of four children. Sibling rivalry didn't reach biblical proportions, but that was because my parents went out of their way to make sure we didn't murder each other. Being the youngest, I know I caused my older siblings a ton of grief. It's a wonder we reached the ages we are with even a modicum of affection for each other. The fact that today we would do almost anything for each other is astonishing.

So, what can be done to make sure sibling rivalry doesn't become a corrosive influence in our lives? We can put love where it isn't expected.

If you love someone, you will be loyal to him no matter what the cost. You will always believe in him, always expect the best of him, and always stand your ground in defending him. 1 Corinthians 13:4-7 (TLB)

"Siblings are the people we practice on, the people who teach us about fairness and cooperation kindness and caring—quite often the hard way." – Pamela Dugdale

If your siblings aren't using the same "playbook," you may learn that the cost of loving someone is sometimes very high. In which case, you may need to take this Scripture to heart:

> *Lay aside bitter words, temper tantrums, revenge, profanity, and insults. But instead be kind and affectionate toward one another. Has God graciously forgiven you? Then graciously forgive one another in the depths of Christ's love.*
>
> EPHESIANS 4:31-32 (TPT)

STEAL SECOND, NEAL

Fifteen-year-old Neal always batted last and always struck out. His cerebral palsy limited his ability to play, but he loved being part of a team. His teammates encouraged him but realized that each at-bat for Neal was a guaranteed out. As the team huddled with their substitute coach, they were shocked when the coach announced that Neal would be the lead-off hitter.

"Are you sure about that?" One of the players questioned.

Putting his arm around Neal's shoulder, the coach walked with him as Neal put on his batting helmet and selected a bat. "Neal, this time, I want you to just stand there and take pitches. No matter how good a pitch looks, don't swing."

Four pitches later, Neal limped toward first base.

"Who's going to pinch-run for him, coach?" One of the players shouted.

"Let's see how he does on his own," the coach replied.

Calling timeout, the coach walked over and whispered to Neal, "On the first pitch, steal second."

"But coach, I am really, really slow."

"Do your best."

As the pitcher lofted the ball toward the plate, Neal started. The catcher caught the ball and just watched as Neal lumbered toward second. When Neal was about ten feet from the bag, the catcher reared back and fired the ball to the second baseman. As the ball whizzed over the second baseman's head, the third base coach started yelling at Neal, "You can make it. Go for third!"

The crowd went wild as the outfielder finally retrieved the overthrow and lobbed the ball toward the third baseman. The ball went wide, and Neal made the turn toward home. The play at the plate was close, but Neal stepped on the plate a millisecond before the catcher applied the tag.

The team lost the game that day, but they all went home feeling like winners.

Like Neal in the above story, we all have limitations, but similar to the coach in the above true story, our Heavenly Father looks beyond our limitations and sees our potential. Not only that, He knows every flaw, every wrinkle, every thought—and he still loves us.

"O Lord, you have examined my heart and know everything about me. You know when I sit down or stand up. You know my thoughts even when I'm far away." Psalm 139:1-2 (NLT)

Would a friend still respect you if he knew your every thought? Would your husband or wife still love you if they knew your every thought? Your *every* thought? God does. He made you, and, as we learn in Psalm 139, his thoughts about you are precious.

You made all the delicate, inner parts of my body and knit me together in my mother's womb. Thank you for making me so wonderfully complex! Your workmanship is marvelous—how well I know it.

How precious are your thoughts about me, O God. They cannot be numbered! I can't even count them; they outnumber the grains of sand! And when I wake up, you are still with me! Psalm 139:13-14, 17-18

Going back to Neal's story: There was a chance Neal would stumble as he tried to steal second base. It was likely he would be tagged out. But the coach knew he could help Neal up, dust him off, and encourage him to try again. Likewise, we stumble and fall. But God is always waiting to lift us up. We need only ask.

The godly may trip seven times, but they will get up again.
But one disaster is enough to overthrow the wicked.

PROVERBS 24:16

D-DOUBLE DARE

As a kid I loved Halloween. Not the scary stuff. Like many kids, I loved Trick or Treat with all the candy. My best friend Billy Sands and I would map out our route, careful to avoid any house that had a reputation for offering more tricks than treats.

One place that was on everybody's "avoid list" was Mrs. Tompkins' house. She was an elderly lady who lived on the corner of 17th Place and D Street. The gossip was that she was a witch.

The words of a gossip are like choice morsels; they go down to the inmost parts. Proverbs 18:8 (NIV)

It was a D-Double Dare that got me to be the first kid to ring Mrs. Tompkins's doorbell. Billy watched from across the street, as I mounted the steps and peeked in the window. I pressed the doorbell. Almost immediately, the door flung open and there was Mrs. Thompkins.

"TTTTrick or TTTreat," I stuttered.

She smiled broadly and said, "Won't you come in?"

I detected the pleasant aroma of freshly baked cookies. When I looked past her into the house, I saw a row of tables lining the hallway. Each had a bowl filled with goodies. I tossed caution to the wind and walked down the hall looking into each bowl, trying to decide which single treat I wanted most. "Take one from each bowl," she said sweetly.

A generous person will prosper; whoever refreshes others will be refreshed. Proverbs 11:25

"Cowabunga, Buffalo Bob!" I thought. "I've hit the motherload." First, I chose an apple, although I must admit the thought of Sleeping Beauty crossed my mind. Then, I grabbed a packet of candy corn, a Hershey bar, a chocolate chip cookie, and a straw filled with pink sugar.

I thanked her and raced back across the street. Billy took one look at my haul, then took off, anxious to see what goodies he would be able to toss into his bag. The word spread quickly. Mrs. Tompkins' house became a "must-see" destination for our neighborhood trick or treaters.

As I look back on this experience, I can't help but wonder how disappointed Mrs. Tompkins would have been if no one had rung her doorbell that night. I don't know who started the gossip that made her place off-limits, but I know gossip could have deprived her of the joy of giving and a whole lot of kids the joy of receiving the treats she had prepared so carefully.

It saddens me when I think back on that Halloween night because I know, as a little boy, I wouldn't have been nearly as enthusiastic about Mrs. Tompkins if she hadn't been so generous. How much of that selfish little boy is still in me? In each of us?

On Halloween, Bonnie and I will once again go trick or treating with our El Segundo grandchildren. El Segundo is a wonderful city in which to trick or treat because the people there offer some serious treats . . . talk about abundance! I will need to suppress that little boy in me who is impressed by abundance and remember to offer the same level of thanks to the man who gives our grandkids a single Hershey kiss as I offer to the candy-philanthropist who gives out share-size bags of M&Ms.

It can be like that in our relationship with God. We can get so used to getting share-sized blessings from God that we take for granted the everyday kisses he sends our way. We need to remember 1st Chronicles 29:16: *LORD our God, all this abundance that we have . . . comes from your hand, and all of it belongs to you.*

UNREQUITED LOVE

The story is told about a kindergardener who changed schools in the middle of the school year. He was having difficulty making friends, so he came up with the idea of giving Valentine's Day cards the kids in his class. His mother helped him prepare thirty-two hand-made cards, one for each child, and a special one for his teacher. The day came, and he went off to school carrying a bag full of cards.

His mother was working in the kitchen when he returned home empty-handed. Fearing the worst, she asked him what had happened at school. He shook his head. "Not a one!" he said. "Not a single one."

His mother was astonished when he suddenly broke into a broad smile. "I didn't forget anyone, he said proudly. "Not a one!" He didn't even give a thought to the fact that no one had remembered to bring a card for the "new kid" in class. The important thing to him was that he had been able to show his love to everyone.

"A new command I give you: Love one another. As I have loved you, so you must love one another. By this everyone will know that you are my disciples, if you love one another." John 13:34-35 (NIV)

That's a humbling standard. It's almost as difficult for me to get my mind around as Matthew 5:48 where Jesus ends his discourse on loving neighbors with the words, *"Be perfect, therefore, as your heavenly Father is perfect."*

In the case of the kindergardener with his valentines, we have a glimpse of what perfect love might look like. His response to unrequited love was pure joy. He did what he did, expecting nothing in return. Sure, he hoped the cards would help him make friends, but he decided the best way to find a friend was to be one.

Easy for a five-year-old, but not always easy for adults. Sometimes the risk of putting oneself out there doesn't seem worth the pain. Maybe, you've been the type of friend Proverbs 18:24 describes as *a friend who sticks closer than a brother.* But you've been disappointed by, or even betrayed by your friend. You've been there through their ups and downs, only to have them walk away when you needed a shoulder to cry on. Unrequited love like that can trigger disappointment that can turn to bitterness that can lead to anger.

Are you angry because someone failed to respond the way you felt they should? It may help you get past your anger to remember that love isn't a quid pro quo virtue. There isn't always a return on investment when you give of yourself. Sure, it's human nature to feel disappointment when someone fails to reciprocate or respond appropriately to your kindness. It is Christ-like to forgive them. God so loved the world . . ..We can requite His love by loving Him and by sharing the love he has given us.

Be kind and compassionate to one another, forgiving each other, just as in Christ God forgave you.

EPHESIANS 4:32

BUILDING CHRIST-LIKE RELATIONSHIPS

A group of Christian men was discussing marriage. "I think I made a big mistake the other night," one of them shared. "My wife and I were having an argument. In frustration, I said, 'I bet 95% of the women in the world would thank God to have a husband like me!' Based on my wife's response," he continued, "I'm afraid she may now be in the 5%."

Once everyone stopped laughing, the discussion turned to ways men can become better husbands. When we think of Scriptures related to marriage, 1st Corinthians 13 comes to mind. But I also encourage men to have an open discussion with their wives about the Scriptures below. Of course, it might be a good idea to first ask yourself, "Do I do this, and if not, why not?

Three Scriptures That Can Change Your Relationships
1st Peter 3:7, Ephesians 5:1-5, Philippians 4:8-9

In the same way, you husbands should live with your wives in an understanding way. You should show respect to them. They are weaker than you. But God gives them the same blessing that he gives you—the grace that gives true life. Do this so that nothing will stop your prayers. 1 Peter 3:7 (ICB)

Am I understanding? Am I respectful? Are we blessed?

You are God's children whom he loves. So try to be like God. Live a life of love. Love other people just as Christ loved us. Christ gave himself for us—he was a sweet-smelling offering and sacrifice to God.

But there must be no sexual immorality among you. There must not be any kind of evil or greed. Those things are not right for God's holy people. Also, there must be no evil talk among you. You must not speak foolishly or tell evil jokes. These things are not right for you. But you should be giving thanks to God. Ephesians 5:1-4

Am I living a life of love? Is my home free of evil? Are my words appropriate? Do I give thanks to God?

Turn to Philippians 4:8-9 whenever you are unsure of the direction to go. Asking yourself, "Is it right? Is it pure? Is it lovely? Is it admirable? Is it praiseworthy?" can help you avoid choosing a path that would be harmful to your relationship.

Finally, brothers and sisters, whatever is true, whatever is noble, whatever is right, whatever is pure, whatever is lovely, whatever is admirable—if anything is excellent or praiseworthy—think about such things. Whatever you have learned or received or heard from me or seen in me—put it into practice. And the God of peace will be with you. Philippians 4:8-9 (NIV)

The beauty of these three Scriptures is they don't only apply to the husband-wife relationship; they apply to all relationships. When we incorporate these actions into our lives, we become more like Christ, and the more Christ-like we become, the stronger all of our relationships will be.

PEOPLE PLEASER OR GOD'S SERVANT?

Am I now trying to win the approval of human beings, or of God? Or am I trying to please people? If I were still trying to please people, I would not be a servant of Christ. Galatians 1:10 (NIV)

Sometimes the desire to make people like or accept us can cause us to make decisions that lead us away from God. Finding the balance between being pleasing to people and being a "people pleaser" can be difficult. This is especially true when the one we are trying to please has a worldview that conflicts with our personal worldview.

Worldview can be defined as how values and beliefs affect the way people, either individually or as part of a group, interpret accumulated information to form opinions on a variety of issues. The Christian worldview is shaped by a belief in the Bible as the Word of God.

As for God, his way is perfect: The Lord's word is flawless; he shields all who take refuge in him. Psalm 18:30

When we get into a discussion with another believer, we share core beliefs that can make our worldviews compatible. Conflict can be avoided by following the dictum repeated by St. Augustine, "In the essentials unity, in non-essentials liberty, and in all things charity,"

If it is possible, as far as it depends on you, live at peace with everyone. Romans 12:18

The issue becomes more difficult when the person we are trying to please has values or beliefs that conflict with our own. What do we do when someone challenges our core beliefs? While there is no rule that requires us to join every argument we are invited to, we can keep in mind the words of the apostle Peter:

But in your hearts revere Christ as Lord. Always be prepared to give an answer to everyone who asks you to give the reason for the hope that you have. But do this with gentleness and respect. 1 Peter 3:15

Of course, there are people who will try to put you down if you dare mention anything about God or Jesus. They will take Bible verses out of context and challenge you to respond to their false presuppositions. They will do everything in their power to make you feel "less than" when you don't have instant responses to their questions. "Why do you believe in fairy tales?" they may ask.

When you encounter this type of person, take heart.

"Blessed are those who are persecuted because of righteousness, for theirs is the kingdom of heaven.

Blessed are you when people insult you, persecute you and falsely say all kinds of evil against you because of me." Matthew 5:10-11

The person without the Spirit does not accept the things that come from the Spirit of God but considers them foolishness, and cannot understand them because they are discerned only through the Spirit. 1 Corinthians 2:14

Bonnie took to heart Jesus' words from Matthew 5:18, "*In the same way, let your light shine before others, that they may see your good deeds and glorify your Father in heaven.*" She clung to her friendship with a non-believing girlfriend for ten years, praying her friend might come to know the Lord.

One day she was attending a luncheon at her friend's house when her friend and another woman began to challenge her for being pro-life. Bonnie had the option of being a people pleaser or to speak up and say something that might end the friendship. Bonnie decided she wanted to be right with God and spoke up.

We are not trying to please people but God, who tests our hearts. 1 Thessalonians 2:4b

Sadly, we sometimes have to say, "Goodbye." The friendship ended, but the door remains open for reconciliation. Bonnie continues to pray that her friend will come to know the Lord.

I tell you that in the same way there will be more rejoicing in heaven over one sinner who repents than over ninety-nine righteous persons who do not need to repent.

LUKE 15:7

COINCIDENCE
OR GOD'S PROVIDENCE

YOU GAVE ME LIFE AND SHOWED ME KINDNESS,
AND IN YOUR PROVIDENCE WATCHED OVER MY SPIRIT.

Job 10:12 (NIV)

SEEDS OF PREJUDICE

Surprisingly, the word *prejudice* is not in the Bible, however, the Bible is full of examples of what we would call prejudice. The open hostility between Jews and Samaritans and between Jews and the gentiles became the backdrop for several of Jesus' parables.

It's natural to notice differences between people. It's how we react to the differences that can lead to sin. Jesus was raised in a culture where the Samaritans were considered second-class citizens, but he rejected the norm and related to the Samaritans in love.

When we generalize and allow the sins of a few to color our opinions of an entire group of people, we are setting ourselves up for God's judgment. A number of verses in the Bible warn us to avoid prejudice.

In Romans we read, *You, then, why do you judge your brother or sister? Or why do you treat them with contempt? For we will all stand before God's judgment seat.* Romans 14:10 (NIV)

And in James: *My dear brothers and sisters, how can you claim to have faith in our glorious Lord Jesus Christ if you favor some people over others?* James 2:1 (NLT)

Then, there is Galatians 3:28: *There is no longer Jew or Gentile, slave or free, male and female. For you are all one in Christ Jesus.*

Allow me to share a personal story about how seeds of prejudice were sown in my life, and what it took to repair the damage. On April 4, 1968, I left my parent's home in Anacostia and drove towards Arlington, Virginia, where I was planning to have supper. My drive took me down Pennsylvania Avenue and across the Sousa Bridge. After taking a slight left on Potomac Avenue, I slowed down as a dark-skinned man, obviously under the influence, stumbled into the roadway and fell. I pulled over, got out of my car, and helped the man to stand and walk to the curb.

Seemingly out of nowhere, a crowd of fifteen or twenty angry people surrounded me. Someone shouted, "He tried to run that man over!" Another screamed, "I saw it, let's teach that "honkey" a lesson." The path to my car was blocked, so I scanned the crowd to see who

I should expect would throw the first punch. Some of the men were carrying sticks and bottles, so I knew I was in serious trouble.

From the midst of the crowd, a middle-aged Afro American cab driver emerged. "Leave him alone!" He shouted. "I saw him helping our brother out of the street." The cab driver turned toward me and in a soft voice asked, "Boy, don't you know what's happened?"

I started to explain, "I was helping . . ."

He interrupted me. "No, man! Get the Hell outta here NOW! Somebody just shot Dr. King."

Somehow, I managed to get back into my car and drive away. Less than an hour later buildings in that area were in flames.

I canceled my supper plans and instead went to a hill, in Arlington, which overlooks Washington. The skyline was aglow from fires that had been ignited around the city. I can't repeat my exact words. Suffice it to say, they were vulgar and hateful. "This is my city, I screamed! I will never forgive THEM!"

That cab driver didn't stereotype me. He didn't care about the color of my skin; he saw me as a fellow human being in trouble. His actions probably saved my life that evening. Sadly, I did not show the same kind of compassion for those who in their anger had burned "my" city.

Few if any of us can honestly say they are not at least a little prejudice. But looking at life through a prism of prejudice can lock us in a prison of negativity. The question facing each of us is, "What can I do to clean out any seeds of prejudice I find in my heart?"

As a start, we can pray God will help us focus on the things we have in common, rather than on things that separate us. God made us all, and any advantage we may have is a gift from God.

For what gives you the right to make such a judgment? What do you have that God hasn't given you? And if everything you have is from God, why boast as though it were not a gift? 1 Corinthians 4:7 (NLT)

Next, we can try to live the Great Commandment. When Jesus told us, "*Thou shalt love thy neighbor as thyself,*" he didn't qualify it. He said, "*Love thy neighbor,*" and we are all neighbors in God's eyes. It's easy to love someone who is like you, but our commitment to Christ can be measured by how we treat those who are different.

How we speak about others can perpetuate negative stereotypes. The apostle James warned us, *With the tongue we praise our Lord and Father, and with it we curse human beings, who have been made in God's likeness.* James 3:9 (NIV)

The apostle Paul encouraged us to build up each other rather than tear each other down. *Let us therefore make every effort to do what leads to peace and to mutual edification.* Romans 14:19

The Psalmist knew we need to watch our words. *Take control of what I say, O Lord, and guard my lips.* Psalm 141:3 (NLT)

If you still struggle with feelings of prejudice, look for a hero. For a long time, the people who set the fires in D.C. were the first ones who came to mind when I thought about Afro-Americans. When I finally replaced the arsonists in my mind's eye with Jim Williams, a compassionate, Christian gentleman—who just happens to be Afro-American—I saw what the love of Christ is all about. The bitterness and fear that fueled my prejudice evaporated in the intensity of Jim's Christian love.

Jim was also the one who taught me the healing power of a smile and (where appropriate) a hug. When you lower your barriers and hug someone, you show them you accept them as they are.

Removing the seeds of prejudice is difficult because pain and fear are efficient fertilizers. An offense by a few can lead us to diminish the value of many. But as Christians, we have been given the ministry of reconciliation. Prejudice erects a barrier that prevents us from fulfilling the task we have been assigned . . . the task of reconciliation.

God has given us this task of reconciling people to him. For God was in Christ, reconciling the world to himself, no longer counting people's sins against them. And he gave us this wonderful message of reconciliation.

2 CORINTHIANS 5:18B-19

THE STORY OF HOPE

We first met Dewi during the summer of 2015 when she joined our Assisted Living Ministry Team at a community in Rancho Santa Margarita, California. Dewi had been a caregiver in this community, so she knew most of the residents. She approached them with such a loving heart; we couldn't help falling in love with her. Since her parents lived far away, my wife Bonnie soon became her U.S. "Mom."

Dewi had been born and raised Muslim in a small town in Indonesia. During high school, she was introduced to Christianity and committed her life to Christ. She met and fell in love with her husband Kris in the small town of Cirebon, Indonesia.

When they married in 2005, there was a period of three years when they saw each other only a couple of times, as Dewi went through the arduous immigration process in preparation for a move to the United States. During one of these visits, Dewi asked Kris, who had been raised Catholic, to join her at a local church service. Dewi was pleasantly surprised when he responded to the altar call and stepped forward to accept Jesus as his Lord and Savior.

After Dewi and Kris settled in California in 2008, they agreed they should concentrate on their education and careers. Fast forward to 2014. Dewi had started praying God would bless her with a child. Moving into 2015, still no pregnancy, Dewi and Bonnie would spend time together after the chapel service praying God would allow Dewi to have a baby.

Sadly, when Dewi and Kris sought help from a fertility clinic, they learned medical conditions diminished the probability they would ever be able to have children. They went through a series of tests and followed recommended procedures, but still no pregnancy.

About this time, Dewi began to question whether God was even hearing her prayers. She surrendered to the possibility that it wasn't God's will that she have a baby and changed her prayer to "Lord, help me to accept your decision."

The next option would have been to take fertility medications, but before going that route, Dewi and Kris decided to take a vacation to Indonesia. On vacation, they did everything she wouldn't be able to do if she were to become pregnant. From mountain biking to water sports, they did it all. When they returned from vacation, they once again visited their fertility specialist. He advised them no further treatment would be necessary. She was already pregnant!

You can't imagine the joy we felt when we learned Dewi was going to have a baby—a baby girl she and Kris had already decided to name "HOPE."

About a month later, Bonnie and I were touring in Alberta, Canada, when Dewi called. We could hear the pain in her voice, as she explained that her doctor had ordered genetic testing, and the tests showed there was a high probability her baby had Turner syndrome, a chromosomal condition that affects the development of females.

"Why has God let this happen?" She asked softly.

We tried to console her but found it difficult to speak through our own tears. We prayed with her over the phone and promised to support her no matter what the outcome.

What followed was a series of what Christian author Squire Rushnell would categorize as "God Winks" — unexpected messages that indicated God's in charge and everything was going to be alright.

God Wink #1: After speaking with Dewi, the next stop on our tour was a gondola ride at Sulfur Mountain in Alberta. As we stood in line waiting for the ride to the top, Bonnie noticed a young man wearing a bright yellow wristband. "Do you see what that says?" She asked. She wanted to buy the band from the young man, but the best she could do was get a photo . . . Hope!

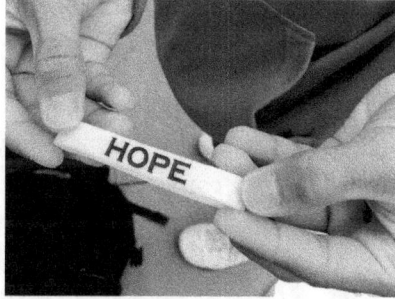

God Wink #2: On the ride down the mountain, we sat behind two young men. "Do you see his tattoo?" Bonnie asked excitedly. "*For I can do everything through Christ, who gives me strength.*" Philippians 4:13 (NLT)

God Wink #3: It was the third "God Wink" that sealed the deal for us. Lake Louise is one of the most beautiful places on Earth. That eve-

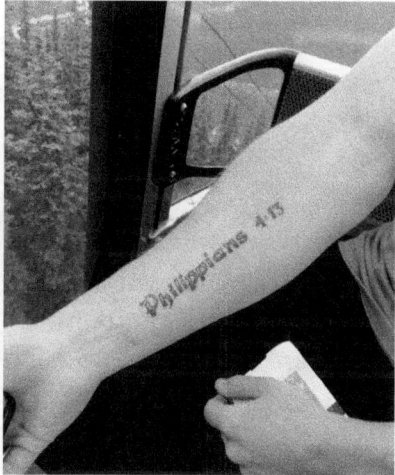

ning, as Bonnie and I walked along the path toward the boathouse, we were wondering out loud how anyone could see something this beautiful and doubt the existence of God. A couple walking in front of us turned toward us; the woman said, "I feel the presence of God in your life. Are you Christians?"

We talked for several minutes about our home churches, ours at Saddleback, theirs at a small parish in Australia. Out of the blue, Bonnie asked the woman, "Would you be willing to pray for our friend Dewi. She really needs prayer."

It deserves mention: Bonnie isn't in the habit of stopping in the middle of a path, grabbing the hands of a couple of strangers, and asking them to pray, but she does believe *The earnest prayer of a righteous person has great power and produces wonderful results.* James 5:16b

I am not skilled enough as a writer to describe the power we felt as this Australian woman prayed. Hers wasn't a cautious appeal; it was a bold conversation with a God she knows intimately. She praised him for who He is. She thanked him for all He has done, then she thanked him for the miracle he would do for Hope. The last words of her prayer were, "That baby will be healed. Amen."

When I returned to our hotel room, I sent an email to Dewi that read in part, "Our hearts are heavy but hopeful. After we spoke to you today, we had a series of experiences that confirmed that God is in charge, and He is aware of your pain.

We put our hope in the Lord. He is our help and our shield.
Psalm 33:20

We can't know what God has in mind when we face trials, but we know he loves you and wants to comfort you. We love you."

Three weeks after we returned from our vacation, Dewi called to tell us a follow-up test revealed the baby was perfectly healthy. We leave it to you to decide if the first test was a false positive or if God had once again responded to prayer.

The next call from Dewi came January 2nd at 10:30 P.M. This time sobs of pain

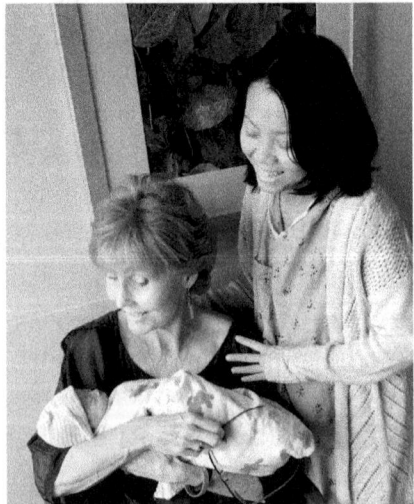

Hope Kirsten was born on January 3, 2017.

were mixed with an unmistakable tone of joy. "I'm in labor . . . and it hurts."

We drove to the hospital and stayed with Dewi and Kris until a nurse advised us it would be morning before Dewi would be ready to deliver. We decided to go home to get some rest. A few hours later, we were awakened by the text tone on my phone. The nurse who had told us it would be OK to go home obviously didn't know God's timing.

And the miracle of Hope has just begun. She will do all things through Christ who strengthens her.

> *Why am I discouraged? Why is my heart so sad?*
> *I will put my hope in God! I will praise him again—*
> *my Savior and my God!*
> Psalm 42:11

Dewi added, "Let the people give glory and honor to Him who is worthy of praise and made this happen."

We asked Dewi to review this story before we sent it to the publisher. This was her response:

"The story brings me back to those days: it fills my heart with joy and praise to our Lord. Looking back and looking at her now, makes my heart sing "How Great Thou Art." Thank you so much for being by my side and for your continuous support 😊🙏. We love you dearly.

On a side note, I was laughing when I read the part when I was in labor, I said, 'It hurts.' Of

By the way, Hope now has a little sister Emily.

course, it hurt, I'm in labor. 😆 I found it funny now. It wasn't funny at all at that time."

WHAT'S ON YOUR BUCKET LIST?

Many years ago, while eating lunch with a client in New Orleans, our conversation turned to the topic of "Bucket Lists." I mentioned to him that my bucket list included a desire to pet a Bengal tiger. On the way back to his office, my client asked me if I was serious about wanting to pet a tiger.

"Dead serious," I replied.

Rather than returning to his office, we drove away from the city into a bayou area, eventually pulling up to a remote site, the offices of Twin Tiger Trucking Company. In the center of the complex, there was a large cage, with two full-grown Bengal tigers.

"Still want to pet a tiger?" He challenged.

"UH! Yep!" I replied.

My client introduced me to the tiger's trainer who took us up to the cage. I got ready to reach in and pet a tiger as it passed. But rather than stopping by the side of the cage, the trainer opened the door and led us inside the cage. "Don't make any quick moves," he cautioned as we gingerly moved to one side of the cage. The larger of the two cats approached and brushed against my leg.

"Don't worry, he's a pussycat," the trainer offered.

Ever so slowly, I reached down and stroked the back of the tiger. I had expected it to be soft and cuddly like a teddy bear, but it was coarse, much like the hair on a deer. As the tiger moved past me and approached my client, she suddenly whipped her head around, opened her mouth, and latched onto my client's leg.

With cat-like speed, the trainer raised a stick he was carrying and yelled, "NO!" The tiger released her grip and raced to the other side of the cage. We rapidly exited the cage. There were bruises on the leg the tiger had bitten, but luckily no major damage.

Getting into a cage with two Bengal tigers doesn't rank among the smartest things I've ever done, but it was a way to achieve one of the goals I had set for myself, and I was willing to trust a total stranger with my life.

A huge question is, "Whom are we willing to trust with our lives? Proverbs 3:5 (NLT) tells us, *Trust in the Lord with all your heart; do not depend on your own understanding.* But trusting in the LORD is sometimes easier said than done. One of the problems we have as finite humans is being able to wrap our minds around the concept of an infinite God—a God who created the universe and everything in it. He's just too big!

"We only hear a small whisper of him. So who can understand God's thundering power?" Job 26:14b (ICB)

We perceive a three-dimensional world—up, down, and sideways. How can we fully understand a being who exists outside of time, a being who has five, ten, or perhaps an infinite number of dimensions? But God wants us to know Him, so He sent His Son Jesus and gave us the freedom to accept or reject him. God wanted us to come to know him because in knowing him, we could learn to love and to trust Him.

Perhaps it's time to update our (Christian) Bucket List:

- *Draw Near to God. Let us draw near to God with a sincere heart and with the full assurance that faith brings, having our hearts sprinkled to cleanse us from a guilty conscience and having our bodies washed with pure water.* Hebrews 10:22 (NIV)
- *Trust in the Lord with all your heart and lean not on your own understanding; in all your ways submit to him, and he will make your paths straight.* Proverbs 3:5-6

- *Be Forgiving. Bear with each other and forgive one another if any of you has a grievance against someone. Forgive as the Lord forgave you.* Colossians 3:13
- *Be Thankful. Therefore, since we are receiving a kingdom that cannot be shaken, let us be thankful, and so worship God acceptably with reverence and awe.* Hebrews 12:28
- *Rejoice in the Lord and be glad, you righteous; sing, all you who are upright in heart!* Psalm 32:11
- **Search the Scriptures** . . . as you add to your own bucket list.

Life, like the tiger in my story, can be unpredictable. Fortunately, God is totally predictable. God said, "*Never will I leave you; never will I forsake you.*" Hebrews 13:5b

We, like the psalmist, can respond: *Therefore we will not fear, though the earth give way and the mountains fall into the heart of the sea,*" PSALM 46:2

*Dedicated to our dear friend, the one-and-only,
Bennye "Wildcat" Rose.*

PROMISE KEPT—SKYDIVING

Thirteen years ago, when my oldest granddaughter was five, I promised to take her skydiving on her eighteenth birthday. Over the ensuing years, I would remind her of the promise. At five, she was clear, jumping out of an airplane wasn't something she'd even consider. At ten, she was adamant; there was no way she would jump out of a perfectly good airplane. By fifteen, she was cautiously enthusiastic. At seventeen, her standard response was, "Don't tell Mom."

July 16th was the big day. I had prepaid for her tandem jump at the skydiving facility. We arrived an hour early to make sure everything was in order. As we were filling out the various waivers, which pretty much say you have no rights whatsoever, Sierra turned to me and asked, "Pop-Pop, how do I answer this question on the form: 'Do you have a heart condition?'"

"Tell the truth," I replied, knowing this answer could put an unwelcome end to our thirteen-year adventure.

Sierra suffers from POTS (postural orthostatic tachycardia syndrome). This is a condition in which a change from a lying position to standing causes an abnormally large increase in heart rate. It is managed through medication and by regularly drinking large amounts of water. We had discussed riding roller coasters and other amusement park rides with her physician. He did not anticipate any problems. The day before and the morning of the jump, we made sure Sierra took her medications and was well hydrated.

When one of the jump masters looked at the form, he immediately said, "You can't jump without a note from your doctor." I was starting to call Kaiser to see if there was any way I could get in touch with her cardiologist when Sierra stepped up and explained her condition to the jumpmaster, "I need to stay hydrated, so I drank a lot of water this morning. My cardiologist even gave me a note so I could get in the short lines for all the rides at Magic Mountain."

"OK . . . You can jump," he said.

Our jump went off without a hitch. Sierra even managed to guide her chute into a standing landing, while my bottom-first landing was less picturesque.

Sierra walked away from our experience having learned two important lessons: First, she learned the importance of keeping commitments. We had promised each other we would skydive on her birthday, and we both lived up to that commitment. Second, she learned that even when your ability to live up to a commitment is in danger, tell the truth.

People with integrity walk safely, but those who follow crooked paths will be exposed. Proverbs 10:9 (NLT)

May integrity and honesty protect me, for I put my hope in you. Psalm 25:21

Although the story had a happy ending, I am troubled because my integrity was challenged and I failed that test. I had to think twice before I told Sierra to tell the truth. The dream was so close to being fulfilled; I wanted to avoid anything that would cause our jump to be canceled. Had Sierra not asked me how she should answer the health question, I wouldn't have said anything. Sierra was the one who showed integrity.

Living a life of integrity means your heart and your head are moving in the same direction, Whenever your heart knows what is right and your head is more concerned with what is right *for you*, you can stray from the way God intends for you to go.

> *God, examine me and know my heart. Test me and know my thoughts. See if there is any bad thing in me. Lead me in the way you set long ago.*
>
> PSALM 139:23-24 (ICB)

WISHING, WORRYING, WHINING, OR WORSHIPING

It was one of those emails you hate to get: "The aortic ultrasound shows no aneurysm, but it did show a possible *growth* in the bladder." What was she thinking? Doesn't my doctor realize that "growth" is one of those medical terms that can conjure up all sorts of disturbing thoughts? For a few minutes, I just sat at my desk wondering how I should process this bit of information. I started worrying about what the implications might be; my fear quickly shifted to whining about how unfair this was.

A verse came to mind: *So we will not fear when earthquakes come and the mountains crumble into the sea.* Psalm 46:2 (NLT)

"OK for you, Mr. Psalmist, but I'm not dealing with an earthquake. I'm dealing with something much more personal." I'm sure many of you have been there. The doctor wants to do a biopsy, or maybe your chest X-ray requires another look. You know God is in control, but at that moment, *you* want to be in control. I needed to be in control, so I did what comes naturally; I went to Google. A plethora of websites that help you self-diagnose popped up. A few clicks of my mouse and I was sure my condition was terminal.

Then, I remembered a message about worry by Pastor Buddy Owen from Saddleback Church. His message was taken from Matthew 6:25-27 (NIV).

"Therefore, I tell you, do not worry about your life, what you will eat or drink; or about your body, what you will wear. Is not life more than food, and the body more than clothes? Look at the birds of the air; they do not sow or reap or store away in barns, and yet your heavenly Father feeds them. Are you not much more valuable than they? Can any one of you by worrying add a single hour to your life?

"When you fix your thoughts on God," Buddy said, "God fixes your thoughts." Then, he offered a simple exercise that can help you fix your thoughts on God rather than on your worries:

If you have something that is troubling you, offer it to the Lord in prayer. Start by praying with your palms up. Imagine your worries are in the palms of your hands. Ask God to take the worries from you. Then, turn your palms down, symbolizing you are letting go of your worries. Finally, turn your palms face up again, as you thank God for the good things he has in store for you.

"OK!" I thought. "This is a good time to try this exercise." Lifting my hands, I imagined my growth sitting in my palms. "Lord, I have a lot to do today, I would appreciate it if you would take care of this worry for me."

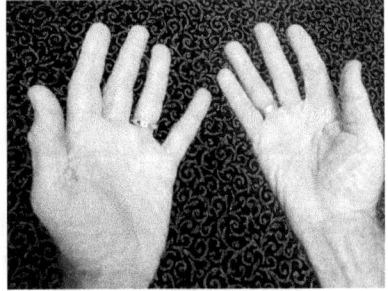

Then, I turned my palms down letting the worry slip from. my grasp. After a brief pause, I lifted my hands and thanked God for His goodness.

Since I was late for an appointment, I rushed to my car and drove away. During my two-hour appointment, concerns about my doctor's email didn't come to mind. Perhaps, I was just too busy to worry. However, as I started my drive home the growth came to mind again. Except, this time it was the memory of a growth I had forgotten.

"Could it be?" I wondered. I called my former urologist and asked if I could pick up a copy of my medical records. When I opened the envelope, I once again saw that word: growth.

I had been through this drill once before. The growth that showed up on my recent MRI was probably the same benign "critter" we had examined a few years ago. Don't get me wrong, this "hands drill" didn't produce a miracle. What it did, in fact, was give me a better way to handle worry.

Later tests revealed I had a very aggressive form of cancer. That cancer was subjected to the same "hands up, hands down, hands up" approach, and I am still thanking God for the successful surgeries I had. That result, I'm convinced, was a miracle.

Scripture tells us, *Cast your cares on the Lord and he will sustain you; he will never let the righteous be shaken.* Psalm 55:22 (NIV)

Cast all your anxiety on him because he cares for you. 1 Peter 5:7

Sometimes the MRI doesn't come out the way we had hoped, or the X-ray brings bad news. Sometimes it just doesn't seem like all things are working together for good. But wishing things could be different, worrying about the implications, and whining because the world isn't fair won't change anything. What will make a difference? Worshipping.

The next time you face a crisis, remember to fix your thoughts on God, so God can fix your thoughts. Perhaps the "growth" you'll have will be spiritual growth.

> *Do not be anxious about anything, but in every situation, by prayer and petition, with thanksgiving, present your requests to God. And the peace of God, which transcends all understanding, will guard your hearts and your minds in Christ Jesus.*
>
> PHILIPPIANS 4:6-7

FROM AGILE TO FRAGILE

Bonnie and I are moving from agile to fragile, and we don't like it a bit! Like us, you may be just waking to the reality of getting older. Alternately, you may be younger than we and think of aging as a "tomorrow" concern. Others may be much older, able to look back at a whole series of unwelcome changes. Whichever, sooner or later, we all see the truth in Bette Davis' assessment: "Getting old ain't for sissies."

We don't have a lot of control over the changes we must face. We do, however, have control over the attitude with which we confront the changes. We can choose to mourn what was, or we can choose to make the most of what will be.

When we first met Eiko, a 95-year young dear friend, we asked her how she liked being in assisted living. She responded, "It was a change, but they feed me, keep my room clean, and offer plenty of activities. What's not to love?"

Each Saturday at the close of the chapel service, Eiko assures us, "I'll see you next week if I'm still here." When she says, "If I'm still here," she means, "If God hasn't called me home." She squeezes as much life as she can from each day, confident that whatever trouble she encounters is little more than a bump in the road that is leading her to heaven.

A Bible verse that seems to apply to our amazing friend's attitude is *Gray hair is a crown of glory; it is gained by living a godly life.* Proverbs 16:31 (NLT)

Another acquaintance of ours isn't nearly as positive. To her, every bump in the road is a boulder. Why the difference? Eiko has something special. Her attitude is shaped by the Spirit of God living within her.

But it is the spirit in a person that gives him understanding. It is the breath of God All-Powerful in him. Job 32:8 (ICB)

"Continue to Grow"

From agile to fragile, it happened so fast.
It's hard to believe how quickly years passed.
You think we are failing; we want you to know:
so long as we're green, we'll continue to grow.
We'll grow and we'll flourish with faith in the Lord,
sustained by the promises found in His Word.

The righteous will flourish like a palm tree, they will grow like a cedar of Lebanon; planted in the house of the LORD, they will flourish in the courts of our God. They will still bear fruit in old age, they will stay fresh and green, proclaiming, "The LORD is upright; he is my Rock, and there is no wickedness in him." Psalm 92:12-15 (NIV)

If you are looking for some spiritual nourishment to help you grow in the Lord, you may appreciate the following Scriptures.

The Lord is the everlasting God, the Creator of all the earth. He never grows weak or weary. No one can measure the depths of his

110

understanding. He gives power to the weak and strength to the power-less. Isaiah 40:28a-29 (NLT)

My grace is all you need. My power works best in weakness. So now I am glad to boast about my weaknesses, so that the power of Christ can work through me. 2 Corinthians 12:9b

The LORD is good to those who depend on him, to those who search for him. So it is good to wait quietly for salvation from the LORD. Lamentations 3:25-26

No, dear brothers and sisters, I have not achieved it, but I focus on this one thing: Forgetting the past and looking forward to what lies ahead, I press on to reach the end of the race and receive the heavenly prize for which God, through Christ Jesus, is calling us. Philippians 3:13-14

The encouraging words below were taken from the book *Mi Vida* by Jose N. Harris.

"There comes a time in your life when you walk away from all the drama and the people who create it. You surround yourself with people who make you laugh. Learn from the bad and focus on the good. Love the people who treat you right and pray for the ones who don't. Life is too short to be anything but happy. Falling down is part of life. Getting back up is living."

The godly may trip seven times, but they will get up again.
But one disaster is enough to overthrow the wicked.

PROVERBS 24:16

WHOSE VOICE
ARE YOU HEARING?

He says, "Be still, and know that I am God;
I will be exalted among the nations,
I will be exalted in the earth."

Psalm 46:10 (NIV)

VOICES IN OUR HEAD

The 2015 Pixar movie *Inside Out* is set in the mind of a young girl, Riley Andersen, where five personified emotions: Joy, Sadness, Fear, Anger, and Disgust try to lead her through life. The film reminds us we aren't the only one who sometimes has nagging voices inside our head.

Most of the time the messages we get are positive and edifying, but there are times when the voices feed us negative thoughts, feelings of inadequacy, or words of condemnation. Those negative thoughts aren't from God! So, how do we filter the negative thoughts that come our way?

Trust in the Lord completely, and do not rely on your own opinions. With all your heart rely on him to guide you, and he will lead you in every decision you make. Proverbs 3:5 (TPT)

Trusting God isn't always easy. At times, we may feel like the father of the demon-possessed boy who brought his son to Jesus for healing.

"Have mercy on us and help us, if you can." The father pleaded.

"What do you mean, 'If I can'?" Jesus asked. "Anything is possible if a person believes."

The father instantly cried out, "I do believe, but help me overcome my unbelief!" Mark 9:22a-24 (NLT)

The father in that story wasn't the only one who struggled with faith. Jesus' disciples had tried and failed to heal the boy. In Matthew we learn, when the disciples asked Jesus why they had failed, he explained, *"You don't have enough faith," Jesus told them. "I tell you the truth, if you had faith even as small as a mustard seed, you could say to this mountain, 'Move from here to there,' and it would move. Nothing would be impossible."* Matthew 17:20

How do we develop that mustard seed of faith? Hebrews 11:1 (NIV) identifies faith as *confidence in what we hope for and assurance about what we do not see.* We can't see gravity, yet we have confidence that if we drop something that is heavier than air it will fall to the ground. Where did that confidence come from? It came from experience; we dropped enough objects to trust the Law of Gravity. Faith in God comes as we learn to trust Him more. We develop that trust by taking the time to do the things that help us know God better.

Read the Bible to discover just who God is.

The discovery phase should never end. My grandmother Alice, who loved and trusted the Lord, had a dog-eared copy of the King James Bible on the armrest of her easy chair. That chair was her sanctuary. She read her Bible faithfully, and she passed that habit on to her children. Finding your own sanctuary and taking time each day to read your Bible can help you come into a more trusting relationship with God.

Expand your prayer life.

Moses, who was afraid to go before Pharoah because of his inability to express himself clearly, had no problem taking his case to God: *Moses said to the Lord, "You have been telling me, 'Lead these people,' but you have not let me know whom you will send with me. You have said, 'I know you by name and you have found favor with me.' If you are pleased with me, teach me your ways so I may know you and continue to find favor with you.* Exodus 33:12-13a

God also knows you by name. When you pray, you open a channel of communication that never has a busy signal. It's as easy as, "Lord, this is me again; let's talk."

Draw closer to God by joining with others in worship.

A community of faith can help its members move into a more loving relationship with God. *And let us not neglect our meeting together, as some people do, but encourage one another, especially now that the day of his return is drawing near.* Hebrews 10:25a (NLT)

What exactly is worship? The Spanish word for worship may be a bit more instructive than the English word. In Spanish, the word is adoración, which is a derivative of the verb "adorer;" which means to adore, to reverence with religious worship, to idolize; to love excessively.

Tune out those negative voices and tune in to God.

When you have a relationship with God, those negative voices we spoke of earlier become easier to silence. Reading the Bible exposes us to heroes of the faith, who teach us to turn to the Lord in times of trouble. Praying and listening for God's response will help us appreciate the many ways God is acting in our lives. Joining with others in worship will also help nurture that mustard seed of faith, that given enough time, will allow us to move what may seem to be the mountains in our life.

> *Make a joyful noise unto the Lord, all ye lands. Serve the Lord with gladness: come before his presence with singing.*
>
> *Know ye that the Lord he is God: it is he that hath made us, and not we ourselves; we are his people, and the sheep of his pasture.*
>
> *Enter into his gates with thanksgiving, and into his courts with praise: be thankful unto him, and bless his name.*
>
> *For the Lord is good; his mercy is everlasting; and his truth endureth to all generations.*
>
> PSALM 100 (KJV)

BUT TO WHOM ARE YOU LISTENING?

How would you feel if you were listening to a sermon when the pastor paused, smiled, then, before he continued his sermon said, "But to whom are you listening? "

Would you be offended? Would you wonder if he thinks his teaching is so powerful that everyone *should* be listening? What if you had *heard* what the pastor was saying, but you hadn't really been *listening*?

Perhaps the pastor realizes hearing is passive, listening is active. Your brain is amazing, but it can't process more than one conscious thought at a time. You can't wrap your thoughts around a discourse on the Sermon on the Mount, for instance, if you are worried about the pork roast you left in the oven. Your mind may flip from the Beatitudes to the pork roast, but you will not be actively listening when your mind is in pork-roast mode.

Another problem is perceptual filters. If we like someone and they are saying things we agree with, almost anything they say is OK. If we don't like them, or if the message touches a sore spot, almost nothing they say will be acceptable. We need only look at the ministry of Jesus to know this is true. Contrast the reaction of those who followed him with the scorn of the Pharisees:

When Jesus had finished saying these things, the crowds were amazed at his teaching. Matthew 7:28 (NIV)

But when the Pharisees heard this, they said, "It is only by Beelzebul, the prince of demons, that this fellow drives out demons." Matthew 12:24

Back to the hypothetical pastor who inserted into his sermon the words, "But to whom are you listening?" It could be he was borrowing from another sermon.

> In Luke 6:20-23 we read, "*Looking at his disciples, he said: 'Blessed are you who are poor, for yours is the kingdom of God. Blessed are you who hunger now, for you will be satisfied. Blessed are you who weep now, for you will laugh. Blessed are you when people hate you, when they exclude you and insult you and reject your name as evil, because of the Son of Man. Rejoice in that day and leap for joy, because great is your reward in heaven. For that is how their ancestors treated the prophets.'*"

At this point, Jesus offered a contrast that may have caused a portion of the crowd to tune out.

> *"But woe to you who are rich, for you have already received your comfort. Woe to you who are well fed now, for you will go hungry. Woe to you who laugh now, for you will mourn and weep. Woe to you when everyone speaks well of you, for that is how their ancestors treated the false prophets"* Luke 6:24-26

Jesus knew that some in the crowd would have stopped "listening" because they had other things on their minds. Others would have tuned out because Jesus had bumped into their perceptual barriers. Jesus knew that even he couldn't hold everybody's attention, so he continued, *"But to you who are listening I say: Love your enemies, do good to those who hate you, bless those who curse you, pray for those who mistreat you."* Luke 6:27-28

Jesus also emphasized the importance of listening when he said, *"So pay attention to how you hear. To those who listen to my teaching, more understanding will be given. But for those who are not listening, even what they think they understand will be taken away from them."* Luke 8:18 (NLT)

In Proverbs we read, *The mind of a smart person is ready to get knowledge. The wise person listens to learn more.* Proverbs 18:15 (ICB)

Romans 10:17 teaches: *So faith comes from hearing the Good News. And people hear the Good News when someone tells them about Christ.*

None of us has perfect hearing, 24-7! Our prayer is that the Holy Spirit will help us to listen more frequently with ears tuned to God's frequency.

God speaks in different ways, and we don't always recognize his voice.

JOB 33:14 (CEV)

ARE YOU USING YOUR CALL BUTTON?

A few years ago, my sister Shirley moved into an assisted living facility where residents can order a "call" button. The device is much more than an emergency response device. Residents can use the button to summon an attendant whenever they need assistance whether for an emergency—such as a fall—or for something as simple as wanting an escort to help them get to the dining room.

GOD has given each of us our own call button: PRAYER.

I call on you, my God, for you will answer me; turn your ear to me and hear my prayer. Psalm 17:6 (NIV)

The question is, "When do we pray?" In 1st Thessalonians 5:16-18, we find the answer: "*Rejoice always, pray continually, give thanks in all circumstances; for this is God's will for you in Christ Jesus.*"

I need to pause at the word "continually." Do I pray continually or just once in a while? Do I give thanks in all circumstances or just when life is going my way?

A few weeks ago, I was driving to LAX to catch a flight back East. I tensed up when I saw the flashing blue lights of a highway patrol cruiser behind me. It turned out, I had swerved out of my lane at one point, and the officer suspected I might be under the influence.

After a few questions, he told me to drive carefully and drove away. As he departed, I noticed the words "To Serve and Protect" on the side of the patrol car. I offered a quick prayer of thanksgiving for the officer. I wonder if I would have offered a prayer of thanksgiving had the officer given me a ticket.

Many of us are not what you would call "prayer warriors." We may know and recite prayers at church; grace at meals may even be a habit, but our most earnest prayers are often reserved for times when we find ourselves in a trouble, or when we acknowledge our sinfulness and plead for mercy.

"The Lord has heard my cry for mercy; the Lord accepts my prayer." Psalm 6:9

God didn't give us prayer as something to do only when all else fails. Our prayer button is available 24-7. From a simple "Thank You" for the day the Lord has given us to a gentle "Now I lay me down to sleep," our days can be sprinkled with prayers. In Ephesians 6:18 the Apostle Paul advises us:

"And pray in the Spirit on all occasions with all kinds of prayers and requests. With this in mind, be alert and always keep on praying for all the Lord's people."

The translation of James 5:13-16 found in the International Children's Bible makes clear the power of prayer:

> *If one of you is having troubles, he should pray. If one of you is happy, he should sing praises. If one of you is sick, he should call the church's elders. The elders should pour oil on him in the name of the Lord and pray for him. And the prayer that is said with faith will make the sick person well. The Lord will heal him. And if he has sinned, God will forgive him. Confess your sins to each other and pray for each other. Do this so that God can heal you. When a good man prays, great things happen.*
>
> *You answer us in amazing ways, God our Savior. People everywhere on the earth and beyond the sea trust you.*
>
> Psalm 65:5

Indeed! When a good man or woman prays, good things happen.

Ready–Set–Pray!

DO YOU EVER TALK TO YOURSELF?

I was sitting in the living room the other day when I thought I heard Bonnie talking in the kitchen. I decided to investigate. Turning the corner, I asked, "Do you need me, or are you just talking to yourself?"

She turned around, smiled, and responded kiddingly, "I am talking to myself, so stop interrupting!"

Do you ever talk to yourself? You're not alone. An article posted on the Live Science website detailed some of the benefits of self-directed speech. "Self-directed speech," the article indicated, "can help guide children's behavior, with kids often taking themselves step-by-step through tasks such as tying their shoelaces, as if reminding themselves to focus on the job at hand."

Researchers also found self-directed speech helped people find objects somewhat more quickly. If talking to myself will help me to learn a new task or to find my missing car keys, it might be worth the potential embarrassment of having people think I'm meshuga [Yiddish for crazy]

I am in the habit of talking-out my problems. When I had to assemble cabinets for the garage, it was very helpful for me to carry on a conversation with myself about which way each board had to be joined to another and which size screw needed to be used with each different type of hardware. What wasn't helpful was when my conversation turned into a self-critique of my very limited mechanical skills.

Next question: Do you ever beat up on yourself with self-directed speech? *Words kill, words give life; they're either poison or fruit— you choose.* Proverbs 18:21 (MSG)

Those who guard their mouths and their tongues keep themselves from calamity. Proverbs 21:23 (NIV)

"If you talked to your friends like you talk to yourself, you wouldn't have any friends." — Mike Cernovich in the book *Gorilla Mindset*

Perhaps we should apply the reverse of the Golden Rule: Do unto yourself as you would have done unto others. Writer Lisa Hayes put it this way, "Be careful how you are talking to yourself because you are listening."

When we hear ourselves muttering negative self-talk, it's time to interrupt. I had one friend who carried 3x5 cards with uplifting Scriptures on them in his pocket. When he felt himself going negative, he would recite the verse from one of his pocket cards over and over until his negative thoughts evaporated.

How precious are your thoughts about me, O God. They cannot be numbered. Psalm 139:17 (NLT)

I can do all things through Christ who strengthens me. Philippians 4:13 (NKJV)

Another form of negative self-directed speech happens when you start talking to your television or your radio. This has become a ubiquitous problem. If you, like me, find yourself "losing it" during the evening news, you might want to consider the following Scriptures:

With the tongue we praise our Lord and Father, and with it we curse human beings, who have been made in God's likeness. Out of the same mouth come praise and cursing. My brothers and sisters, this should not be. James 3:9-10 (NIV)

Understand this, my dear brothers and sisters: You must all be quick to listen, slow to speak, and slow to get angry. James 1:19 (NLT)

Anyone who is never tempted to use negative speech is truly blessed. Some of us need to repent and guard our thoughts; often they find their way into our speech. One antidote may be found in Philippians:

And now, dear brothers and sisters, one final thing. Fix your thoughts on what is true, and honorable, and right, and pure, and lovely, and admirable. Think about things that are excellent and worthy of praise.

PHILIPPIANS 4:8

PAINTING OUR OWN SELF PORTRAIT

God gives us all a canvas; we paint it as we choose.
It isn't Paint by Numbers, nor paint it wrong, "you lose."
We're free to choose our pallet—the thickness of our strokes,
sweeping strands of color, or spots from careless pokes.
And when we feel we're failing and cast our paints aside,
there is a Master Artist who wants to be our guide.
He'll take our feeble efforts if we will just release,
and guided by His steady hand, we'll be His masterpiece.

For we are God's masterpiece.
He has created us anew in Christ Jesus,
so we can do the good things
he planned for us long ago.

EPHESIANS 2:10 (NLT)

FORGIVE AND REMEMBER

FOR I WILL FORGIVE THEIR WICKEDNESS AND
WILL REMEMBER THEIR SINS NO MORE.

Hebrews 8:12 (NIV)

ERASING YOUR MENTAL ETCH A SKETCH®

Do you remember the Etch-A-Sketch® we played with as children? You could scribble anything you wanted on them, then, with a shake of the tablet or a twist of the wheel, erase what been had written and start again.

Unfortunately, it takes more than a shake or a twist to erase our negative thoughts. Memories of how we have been hurt by others or thoughts of how we have intentionally, or accidentally hurt others can leave deep emotional scars. How, we wonder, can we obtain a *tabula rasa*, a clean slate, a mind not troubled by old experiences, guilt, or pain?

Clearing the slate involves forgiveness. It starts with the words of Jesus in the Lord's Prayer: "*And forgive us our debts, as we also have forgiven our debtors.*" Matthew 6:12 (NIV)

Matthew Henry's Commentary explains, "This is not a plea of merit, but a plea of grace. Note: those that come to God for the forgiveness of their sins against him, must make conscience [the inner sense of what is right or wrong in one's conduct or motives, impelling one toward right action] forgiving those who have offended them."

Sometimes we have been hurt so badly we cry, "Do you not know what they have done to me?" Jesus' response might be, "Do you not know what I have done for you?"

Be gentle and ready to forgive; never hold grudges. Remember, the Lord forgave you, so you must forgive others. Colossians 3:13 (TLB)

I don't know about you, but sometimes I hang onto guilt like a dog fighting for a bone. I know that confession, telling God what he already knows about us, is a starting point in erasing negative thoughts. I also believe 1st John 1:9 (NIV): *If we confess our sins, he is faithful and just and will forgive us our sins and purify us from all unrighteousness.* Nevertheless, it can still be a challenge for me to forgive myself. Ever feel that way?

Digging for answers, I read Proverbs 28:13: *Whoever conceals their sins does not prosper, but the one who confesses and renounces them finds mercy.*

We are told to confess and renounce our sins. Repentance is a commitment to feel and show that you are sorry for something you did that offended God and that you sincerely want to do what is right. Try to remember: "If you say you're sorry and keep doing what you're doing, the "I'm sorry" has no value.

In 2nd Corinthians, we are cautioned about the difference between "true" repentance and "worldly sorrow". *Being sorry in the way God wants makes a person change his heart and life. This leads to salvation, and we cannot be sorry for that. But the kind of sorrow the world has will bring death.* 2 Corinthians 7:10 (ICB)

It is important to make sure our "repentance" is prompted by our grief over how we have offended God, not just remorse over the immediate consequences of our actions.

Recently, I heard a pastor say that confessing your sins to someone you trust can help you to heal. That's biblical: *Therefore confess your sins to each other and pray for each other so that you may be healed. The prayer of a righteous person is powerful and effective.* James 5:16 (NIV)

Of course, we should carefully choose the person we confide in.

A gossip betrays a confidence, but a trustworthy person keeps a secret. Proverbs 11:13

In our confessing, we also need to avoid being like the thief who is compelled to return to the scene of the crime. If we repeatedly return to thoughts of past sins, it's time to ask the Holy Spirit to help us forgive ourselves, and trust that God has already forgiven us.

"Come now, let us settle the matter," says the LORD. "Though your sins are like scarlet, they shall be as white as snow; though they are red as crimson, they shall be like wool." Isaiah 1:18

It's simplistic to think we can just forgive and forget. It's something sublime when, with God's help, we can forgive and move on.

HE DROPPED THE BALL

Have you ever heard anyone use the expression, "He dropped the ball?" That expression has an interesting history. In the 1941 World Series of Baseball, the powerful New York Yankees played against their cross-town rivals the Brooklyn Dodgers. That's right L.A. fans—the Dodgers used to play in Brooklyn, NY.

The Dodgers were trailing two games to one, but in game four, things seemed to be turning in the favor of the Dodgers. It was the bottom of the ninth. The Dodgers had a four-runs to three advantage with two out, two strikes on the batter, and no runners on base for the Yankees. One strike away from victory!

The Dodgers' pitcher threw a sharply breaking curveball that should have been the final strike on Yankee's batter Tommy Heinrich, but the Dodger's victory slipped away as the ball caromed off catcher Mickey Owen's glove and skidded to the backstop. Heinrich was able to steal first-base on Owen's error. The Yankees rallied and won the game 7-4. The next day, the Yankees went on to win the World Series.

Do you want to know something interesting about the catcher Mickey Owen? Mickey Owen's .995 fielding percentage in 1941 was a record for fielding efficiency - a record that still stands today! Mickey Owens approached perfection in fielding, and yet, one mistake soiled his entire legacy. When he died, one newspaper's obituary read, "Mickey Owen - The Man who dropped the ball."

Do you sometimes feel as if one mistake, one bad decision, or one wrong choice will end up defining your legacy? Do you wonder if you will be remembered for the good you did or as just another man or woman who "dropped the ball?"

One of the benefits of studying the Bible is that you discover that "dropping the ball" doesn't define your legacy in God's eyes. As we read in Romans, *For all have sinned and fall short of the glory of God, and all are justified freely by his grace through the redemption that came by Christ Jesus.* Romans 3:23-24 (NIV)

Abraham lied (Genesis 20). Jacob deceived his father and stole his brother Esau's inheritance (Genesis 25). David committed adultery with Bathsheba and had her husband Uriah murdered (2nd Samuel). Peter Denied Christ (Matthew 26), and Paul persecuted the church (Acts 9). But as we read the stories of each of these heroes of the faith, we learn God is a God of second chances. Isn't it reassuring to know God doesn't define us based on our mistakes; he loves and accepts us even when we "drop the ball."

And I am convinced that nothing can ever separate us from God's love. Neither death nor life, neither angels nor demons, neither our fears for today nor our worries about tomorrow— not even the powers of hell can separate us from God's love. No power in the sky above or in the earth below—indeed, nothing in all creation will ever be able to separate us from the love of God that is revealed in Christ Jesus our Lord.

ROMANS 8:38-39 (NLT)

WHY CAN'T I FORGIVE MYSELF?

A dear friend asked, "Are there any verses in the Bible that deal with forgiving yourself? I know there are verses that speak about God's love and His willingness to forgive our sins, but I struggle with forgiving myself, with letting go of the shame I feel. Does God want me to remember every bad thing I've ever done?"

"Could it be?" I asked, "You are confusing forgiving with forgetting Forgiving is not about forgetting; it is about remembering with understanding.

"Are you, today, the same person you were then? If you are in Christ, the answer is no; you are not the same. Circumstances change as do people."

Therefore, if anyone is in Christ, the new creation has come: The old has gone, the new is here! 2 Corinthians 5:17 (NIV)

Forgiveness is also about trust. When you read John 3:16 remember YOU are included in the world he came to save. *For God so loved the world that he gave his one and only Son, that whoever believes in him shall not perish but have eternal life,*

Do you really trust that God sent His Son into the world to save YOU? Jesus is our lead attorney.

We have an advocate with the Father–Jesus Christ, the Righteous One. He is the atoning sacrifice for our sins, and not only for ours but also for the sins of the whole world. 1 John 2:1b-2

Notice the words "free from all blame" in the verses from 1st Corinthians which follow.

Now you have every spiritual gift you need as you eagerly wait for the return of our Lord Jesus Christ. He will keep you strong to the end so that you will be free from all blame on the day when our Lord Jesus Christ returns. God will do this, for he is faithful to do what he says, and he has invited you into partnership with his Son, Jesus Christ our Lord. 1 Corinthians 1:7-9 (NLT)

God forgives our sins. Still, there are consequences we must live with. The man or woman who steals may have to go to jail. The person who gossips may be ostracized by others who fear the loose tongue. The husband or wife who divorces may have to endure the wrath of the family.

But there is a time for forgiveness. When someone in the Church at Corinth upset the congregation, the apostle Paul cautioned: *The punishment inflicted on him by the majority is sufficient. Now instead, you ought to forgive and comfort him, so that he will not be overwhelmed by excessive sorrow.* 2 Corinthians 2:6-7 (NIV)

The excessive sorrow Paul wrote about could include an inability to forgive oneself.

Bear with each other and forgive one another if any of you has a grievance against someone. Forgive as the Lord forgave you. Colossians 3:13 "Forgive [yourself] as the Lord forgave you" is one way to look at this verse.

Sometimes our inability to forgive ourselves is caused by how others respond to our pleas for forgiveness. I [Don] once attended a prayer service at an evangelical Episcopal church. The sermon was based on James 5:16: *Therefore confess your sins to each other and pray for each other so that you may be healed. The prayer of a righteous person is powerful and effective.*

Following the sermon. the rector asked the worshipers to confess a sin to someone nearby. A woman seated next to me listened as I gave the details of a sin that had been burdening me. The shocked look on her face and her swift departure from the sanctuary did not help me with my need for self-forgiveness.

Many years later, I was counseled by someone who was more compassionate, more willing to help me look at my sin as the Bible says God looks at it. I confessed, accepted my guilt, and put my trust in the blood of Jesus. I still think of it from time to time, but the memory of my sin no longer causes me the pain it once did.

Unfortunately, those directly impacted by sin sometimes respond by withholding forgiveness as a bargaining chip to get their needs met. Their forgiveness becomes contingent upon your compliance. Scripture tells us we need not let their opinions intimidate us.

Therefore, there is now no condemnation for those who are in Christ Jesus. Romans 8:1

On our own, we may feel what we did was so bad God could never forgive us; we need to remember that God doesn't grade on the curve.

This righteousness is given through faith in Jesus Christ to all who believe. *There is no difference between Jew and Gentile, for all have sinned and fall short of the glory of God, and all are justified freely by his grace through the redemption that came by Christ Jesus.* Romans 3:23-24

Sometimes forgiveness is slow in coming. Days, months, even years later, suddenly you no longer feel guilty. A weight is lifted from your soul—a true gift from the Holy Spirit. God doesn't want us to hold onto painful memories. When we learn to focus more on Christ and less on our faults, shame can be replaced by a strong desire to enter into God's glorious presence. What a joyful day that will be.

> *Now all glory to God, who is able to keep you from falling away and will bring you with great joy into his glorious presence without a single fault.*

JUDE 1:24 (NLT)

GOT GUILT?

A severe case of pneumonia landed me in the hospital. It took about a week of antibiotics and breathing treatments to get to the point where I could return home. Even then, the effects of the infection limited what I could do without tiring. When, after several weeks, my energy level remained low, I made an appointment to see my physician Dr. Wu.

I hate whining, but I felt like whining when I finally got to see the doctor. Laboring to get each word out, I began, "Doc, I had pneumonia weeks ago, and I still struggle to get through the simplest of tasks. How long before I begin to feel better?"

The doctor placed the stethoscope against my chest and listened intently for about a minute. Then, looking me straight in the eye, he raised his right hand, made the peace sign, brought the pointer finger and the middle finger together, and thumped me as hard as he could in the middle of my forehead. "Get over it! You are fine!" Then he turned and walked out of the room. That evening, I went out and played two sets of tennis.

Psychiatrists might say I had been suffering from an anxiety disorder. My mind had become accustomed to feeling poorly, and it took a thump on my forehead to awaken me to the fact I was OK. Guilt is another anxiety disorder. It can be an overwhelming burden when we try to handle it on our own. King David wrote, *My guilt overwhelms me–it is a burden too heavy to bear.* Psalm 38:4 (NLT)

The antidote for guilt is well known to followers of Christ: *"Come to me, all you who are weary and burdened, and I will give you rest. Take my yoke upon you and learn from me, for I am gentle and humble in heart, and you will find rest for your souls. For my yoke is easy and my burden is light."* Matthew 11:28-30 (NIV)

As I was reading this Scripture, I noticed something I had overlooked. Jesus did not say, "I'll take your yoke." He said, "Take my yoke." In other words, leave behind the yoke you have been carrying (the life you have been living and the guilt you have been carrying) and find rest in your new life in Christ. Any guilt you've been carrying was part of an old life. You are living a new life. Hanging onto guilt, a friend suggested, is resurrecting the dead.

This means that anyone who belongs to Christ has become a new person. The old life is gone; a new life has begun! 2 Corinthians 5:17 (NLT)

If you are still carrying the burden of guilt, you might have a trust issue. You can find freedom from guilt by trusting the Lord. He is quicker to forgive you than you can forgive yourself.

In 1st John, we read, *But if we confess our sins to him, he is faithful and just to forgive us our sins and to cleanse us from all wickedness.* 1 John 1:9

What about the sin the "new me" committed yesterday? Shouldn't I feel guilty about that one? Convicted is a more appropriate word than guilty. *Those who are dominated by the sinful nature think about sinful things, but those who are controlled by the Holy Spirit think about things that please the Spirit.* Romans 8:5 (NLT)

Convicted by the power of the Holy Spirit living within us, with a true desire to repent, we don't have to spend our lives looking in the rear-view mirror.

> *The LORD is compassionate and gracious, slow to anger,*
> *abounding in love. He will not always accuse, nor will he*
> *harbor his anger forever; he does not treat us as our sins*
> *deserve or repay us according to our iniquities. for as high as*
> *the heavens are above the earth, so great is his love for those*
> *who fear him; as far as the east is from the west, so far has he*
> *removed our transgressions from us.*
>
> PSALM 103:8-12 (NIV)

MOVE PAST THE PAST

For you created my inmost being; you knit me together in my mother's womb. I praise you because I am fearfully and wonderfully made; your works are wonderful, I know that full well. Psalm 139:13-14 (NIV)

We may read Psalm 139 and wonder what happened between the time we were born and now. We started out with so much potential, but somewhere along the way, we picked up a basketful of bad habits, a brain full of foul memories, and an abundance of regrets. We became human!

We became the poster child for the saying "the here-and-now is about the there-and-then." Past mistakes and past hurts have taken up permanent residency in our brains and come to our mind at the most inconvenient times. Is there anything we can learn from the experience of others that will help us forget our past hurts?

Recently, I heard the testimony of a woman in her early sixties who had suffered from chronic depression. One day as she was praying, she remembered a seemingly small but in fact life-changing incident that had occurred when she was in kindergarten. She had been talking too much in class. Suddenly the teacher grabbed her by the arm and pulled her over to a tall stool. She lifted her onto the stool and placed a dunce cap on her head.

"It was like a movie playing in my head." the woman explained. "I could hear the teacher's voice and feel the hard stool I was sitting on. I could see the faces of the other children laughing at me. Suddenly, this mental video changed. Jesus walked into the room and there was a warm glow around him. As he started walking toward me, the teacher shouted at him, 'Don't!'

"Jesus looked directly at her. Calmly he said, 'You be quiet,' and walked toward me. He hugged me and placed a golden crown on my head. He then handed me additional gold crowns and told me to give them to any other children who needed them. I felt a calm I had never known. Then, my mental video ended. The pain of that kindergarten incident had affected me throughout my life, but God had given me a way to finally move past it."

You remember the story of Joseph, the one with the coat of many colors. He sure had things that could have sent him off the deep end. His parents spoiled him. His brothers hated him and were about to kill him, choosing instead to sell him into slavery.

How did he react? He turned to God for help. Joseph asked the Lord to help him forget his past. If you read the full account in Genesis, you will discover Joseph didn't forget the incidents of the past; he forgot the pain of those incidents. His "here-and-now" became more important than his "there-and-then."

Joseph named his firstborn Manasseh and said, "It is because God has made me forget all my trouble and all my father's household." Genesis 41:51

Job was someone else who had more than his share of problems. You know the story. He lost everything, yet his devotion to the Lord enabled him to forget his troubles.

"Yet if you devote your heart to him and stretch out your hands to him, if you put away the sin that is in your hand and allow no evil to dwell in your tent, then, free of fault, you will lift up your face; you will stand firm and without fear. You will surely forget your trouble, recalling it only as waters gone by." Job 11:13-16

We are encouraged to follow the example of the apostle Paul who shed regrets of his past and kept his eye on what lay ahead. Paul wrote, *Brothers and sisters, I do not consider myself yet to have taken hold of it. But one thing I do: Forgetting what is behind and straining toward what is ahead, I press on toward the goal to win the prize for which God has called me heavenward in Christ Jesus.* Philippians 3:13-14

Are you taking steps to move past the past, or is that old video still playing in your head? Ask Jesus to help you change the picture.

"Right thinking begins with the words we say to ourselves." —James Allen

So keep your thoughts continually fixed on all that is authentic and real, honorable and admirable, beautiful and respectful, pure and holy, merciful and kind. And fasten your thoughts on every glorious work of God, praising him always. Philippians 4:8 (TPT)

"One Rule for Life"

One rule for life – a simple one:
try not to say, "I should have done."
The things you've done, both right and wrong,
are in the past where they belong.
Each day, just pray that through God's
grace you'll show the world a kinder face.
A softer voice, a loving touch
are gifts to God who gave so much.
He gave His son to take your place,
your sins forgive, your shame erase.
As far as East is from the West,
to hide your worst, He gave His best.
The things you've done, both right and wrong
are in the past where they belong.

Want more joy in your life? Remember how far God's forgiveness extends.

For as high as the heavens are above the earth, so great is
his love for those who fear him; as far as the east is from the
west, so far has he removed our transgressions from us.

PSALM 103:11-12 (NIV)

THE VIEW FROM OUR PEW

I APPEAL TO YOU, BROTHERS AND SISTERS,
IN THE NAME OF OUR LORD JESUS CHRIST, THAT ALL
OF YOU AGREE WITH ONE ANOTHER IN WHAT YOU SAY
AND THAT THERE BE NO DIVISIONS AMONG YOU,
BUT THAT YOU BE PERFECTLY UNITED
IN MIND AND THOUGHT.

1 Corinthians 1:10 (NIV)

"The Pastor Selection Committee"

You called for a pastor to shepherd your flock.
Back came the answer, "We have none in stock."
We have preachers and teachers and orators and such,
but a pastor who's a shepherd? You're asking too much.

We have several good leaders; you know that is true,
but nary a one who can look after you.
The church is a pasture where dangers abound,
where wolves in sheep's clothing too often are found.

You're seeking a shepherd, perhaps that is wise.
we're seeking solutions – can you compromise,
and choose from our roster of men of good deeds?
Perhaps one of them will meet all your needs.

We have some who love Jesus, and some who love folks.
There are some who give sermons, while others tell jokes.
Some have great voices with resonant tone,
while others should only sing when they're alone.

But a pastor, a shepherd, who longs to serve God?
That kind of request is really quite odd.
But pray for God's guidance and maybe you'll find
the pastor, the shepherd that you have in mind.

"Humor is a prelude to faith and laughter is the beginning of prayer" – Reinhold Niebuhr

WELCOMING A NEW PASTOR

The search team has scoured the country looking for the perfect candidate. The nominating committee has interviewed the candidates and made its recommendation. The congregation has voted, and the offer has been made. Now, everyone must pray that the person selected will be a shepherd who can help the congregation discern and fulfill God's will.

Working on this book over the past few years has taught us a humbling lesson: serving the Lord isn't always easy. At times, it takes Bonnie and me several hours to grind out a simple two-page devotional. Think about how many more hours are required for your pastor to develop a thirty to forty-five-minute (or more) sermon each week.

Add to that the time and emotional energy it must require to comfort the sick, counsel the oppressed, and conduct the day to day business involved in running a church—all of this while living up to the standard the apostle Paul set forth in First Timothy: *So a church leader must be a man whose life is above reproach. He must be faithful to his wife. He must exercise self-control, live wisely, and have a good reputation. He must enjoy having guests in his home, and he must be able to teach.* 1 Timothy 3:2 (NLT)

Over the years, we have been blessed to have had exposure to some great preachers/teachers: Billy Graham, J. Vernon McGee, Chuck Swindoll, Bishop Fulton Sheen, Robert H. Schuller, Beth Moore, T.D. Jakes, Joyce Meyer, Rick Warren, Timothy Keller, Max Lucado . . . to name a few.

As you read each of these names, what thoughts came to your mind? My guess is that some of the names brought back memories of lessons you have learned, while others may have made you feel uncomfortable. These are people that touched thousands, if not millions with their teaching, yet they don't appeal to everyone.

When you bring it down to the church level, it becomes even more striking. From the rector at the Episcopal church, I attended as a child, all the way down to the seminary candidate who preached at a church Bonnie and I attended a few weeks ago, some speakers have sent me from church wanting to know what God wanted me to learn from the message, while others have sent me seeking a different place to worship.

In his farewell sermon, Randy Steele, former pastor of Laguna Hills Presbyterian Church put the issue in perspective when he said, "I was not as good a pastor as some of you thought I was, nor as bad as others believed.

To quote Shakespeare, "The fault, dear Brutus, is not in our stars, but in ourselves." Too often we can be looking for the shepherd's "S" on a pastor's chest rather than the Spirit in his heart. There is no perfect shepherd, save Jesus Christ.

We can only pray that our pastors will . . . *Preach the word of God. Be prepared, whether the time is favorable or not. Patiently correct, rebuke, and encourage your people with good teaching—and— Through the power of the Holy Spirit who lives within us, carefully guard the precious truth that has been entrusted to you.* 2 Timothy 4:2, 2 Timothy 1:14

As members of the church (with apologies to JFK), let us ask not what our pastors can do for us, let us ask what we can do for our pastors.

JOYFUL, JOYFUL

Make a joyful noise unto the Lord, all ye lands. Serve the Lord with gladness: come before his presence with singing. Psalm 100:1-2 (KJV)

When you survey the Scriptures, you find joy is often associated with shouting and with singing. Having served in the Marine Corps, I am proficient when it comes to shouting, but singing is another matter. That's why what happened to Bonnie and me on our first visit to Laguna Niguel Presbyterian Church caught me off guard.

The service was wonderful. We enjoyed the atmosphere of the church, the sermon was Bible-based and insightful, and the choir was excellent. As we were leaving, we were talking about returning the next Sunday. Then, I saw a middle-aged man in a choir robe running in our direction. I stepped aside to give him room. Instead of running past, he stopped, and reached out his hand, "My name is "Binh (pronounced Bing). Would you like to join our choir?"

Bonnie smiled broadly as she looked at me. That smile sometimes gets me in trouble, so I quickly responded to Binh, "Let me give you three reasons why it's not a good idea for us to join your choir."

"Reason one: This is our first visit; we aren't members of this church.

Reason two: "We can't read music."

With three fingers raised, I confessed reason three: "We can't sing!"

"No problem," Binh said. "You smile, and we need smiling faces."

In her inimitable fashion, Bonnie interjected, "Maybe we could lip-sync for Jesus." We joined the choir and soon learned why joy and singing are so firmly linked.

The Lord is my strength and my shield; my heart trusts in him, and he helps me. My heart leaps for joy, and with my song I praise him. Psalm 28:7 (NIV)

Let the fields be jubilant, and everything in them; let all the trees of the forest sing for joy. Psalm 96:12

Let the rivers clap their hands, let the mountains sing together for joy. Psalm 98:8

When you hear a song, do you focus on the lyrics or just enjoy the melody? Sometimes the best sermons can be in the songs. Consequently, I started paying special attention to the lyrics.

When our choir was preparing to sing "Ode to Joy" at a Christmas Worship Festival, I noticed the lyrics were not particularly, for want of a better word, "Chistmassy"

Ludwig Von Beethoven adapted the words of a non-religious poem "An die Freude," by Friedrich Schiller, as part of the lyrics for the finale (chorale) movement of his Ninth Symphony. In 1907, American author Henry Van Dyke wrote a poem that became the lyrics to the English hymn "Joyful, Joyful We Adore Thee."

Both the German and English versions are often used as part of Christmas cantatas, although neither specifically mention the birth of Christ. With this omission in mind, I drafted a reprise that

Binh included in the Christmas Worship Festival in 2014. It gives me great joy to offer these words to you.

Reprise to "Ode to Joy"

Joyful, joyful, we are joyful.
Celebrate the Savior's birth.
God's own Son was sent to save us;
brought Good News to all on Earth.
From his cradle to Golgotha,
Jesus came to bear our sin.
Open wide the gates of heaven;
all who love him enter in.

This is real love—not that we loved God, but that he loved
us and sent his Son as a sacrifice to take away our sins.

1 JOHN 4:10 (NLT)

FIRST AID KIT FOR CHRISTIANS

Recently, Bonnie and I took a Red Cross first aid course. The instructor taught us that the first step in first aid is to make sure the area is safe before rendering assistance. She emphasized the importance of dialing 9-1-1 and spoke about the legal requirement to obtain permission before touching a conscious victim.

She then taught the proper way to administer the Heimlich maneuver, CPR, and wound care. As she was finishing the section on wound care, she asked, "What would you do if you were walking down the street and noticed someone who was trimming the grass accidentally cut off their big toe?" To add emphasis, she tossed a bloody, plastic toe on the floor.

When no one responded to her question, she explained that you should place the toe in a plastic bag with egg white, whole milk, or coconut milk; mark the person's name, the date and time on the bag, and make sure it gets to the hospital with the victim.

One student raised his hand. "I don't normally carry plastic bags or a magic marker when I walk. Finding milk or egg whites might be difficult. Wouldn't it be easier to just call a TOE truck?"

Don't worry. I've decided to keep my day job and not become a stand-up comic. Since the "tow truck" story really happened, I thought you might enjoy a bit of levity.

On a more serious note, it would be helpful if churches offered a first aid course and a first aid kit for Christians who want to help a brother or sister in Christ who struggles with doubts. As with the Red Cross first aid course, the first step might be to make sure the area is safe.

Check to make sure you are prepared to proceed with love, faith, and mercy.

Pray: *LORD, don't hold back your tender mercies from me. Let your unfailing love and faithfulness always protect me.* Psalm 40:11 (NLT)

Then, make sure you're confident in your faith. It may be wise to check in with your spiritual 9-1-1: a pastor, a deacon, or another Christian brother or sister.

Next, ask yourself, "Can I listen non-judgmentally, guided by love?

Be humble and gentle. Be patient with each other, making allowance for each other's faults because of your love. Ephesians 4:2 (TLB)

"May I help?" is a gentle way to begin. Sometimes people want or even need to work things out on their own. Grief, anger, fear or embarrassment may prevent a free flow of communication. If you find they are open to your involvement, remember: listening is often more healing than your words. Let *them* talk.

Avoid Band-Aid answers. Not everyone is in a place where they are ready to accept "All things work together for good." Ask the

Holy Spirit to guide you as you prayerfully walk with them through their issues.

Be quick to admit you don't have all the answers. Be willing to help them search the Scriptures and books from Christian authors who have looked carefully at the issues. There is a list of resources at the back of this book.

Don't give up. *And I am certain that God, who began the good work within you, will continue his work until it is finally finished on the day when Christ Jesus returns.* Philippians 1:6 (NLT)

Is your spiritual first aid kit packed and ready? Are you prepared to show your heart for Jesus by learning how to help others know *the grace of the Lord Jesus Christ, the love of God, and the fellowship of the Holy Spirit?* 2 Corinthians 13:14a (NIV)

Always be prepared to give an answer to everyone who asks you to give the reason for the hope that you have. But do this with gentleness and respect. 1 PETER 3:15B

"The Preacher with an iPad"

A preacher with an iPad dared preach for us today.
He hadn't memorized his talk; he stood and read away.
He flipped the screen adroitly and never lost his place,
and yet it seemed so very wrong; he waved it in our face.
He knows that we aren't techno-Geeks; we even have landlines,
and yet he trusts that do-dad thing—it really blows our minds.
If he just had a heart for us, he'd toss that cursed pad.
He'd learn from Pastor (you know whom) that paper's not that bad.
He'd write his sermons longhand, six pages double spaced.
If he'd do that, we're pretty sure that he would be embraced.
But if he plans to keep his pad, then, take it straight from me,
that Apple®-packin' preacher better find another tree.

The poem above is a tongue-in-cheek advisory to pastors who find themselves serving an older congregation. We older folks sometimes have a hard time accepting changes; give us time to adjust. By the way, Bonnie and I now bring our smartphones to church to follow Scripture cited in the sermon. So much for our self-righteous indignation.

> *I have become all things to all people so that by all possible means I might save some.*

1 CORINTHIANS 9:22B (NIV)

MORE THAN A PEW TATER

But the Holy Spirit produces this kind of fruit in our lives: love, joy, peace, patience, kindness, goodness, faithfulness, gentleness, and self-control. There is no law against these things! Galatians 5:22-23 (NLT)

What is "goodness"? An excellent synonym is "beneficence": the doing of active goodness, kindness, or charity—including all actions intended to benefit others.

God is not only a "do as I *say*" God; he is also a "do as I *do*" God. When He speaks to us through the Scriptures, His message is, "Love because I love. Be patient because I am patient. Be kind because I am kind. Do good because I do good. Have mercy because I have mercy."

The apostle Paul makes it clear in his letter to Titus that we should use our lives for doing good, not to earn God's mercy; we already have that in Jesus. Rather, we use our lives for doing good as a form of thanksgiving for God's mercy and grace.

> *But then the kindness and love of God our Savior was shown. He saved us because of his mercy, not because of good deeds we did to be right with God. He saved us through the washing that made us new people. He saved us by making us new through the Holy Spirit.*
>
> *The letter continues: This teaching is true. And I want you to be sure that the people understand these things. Then those who believe in God will be careful to use their lives for doing good. These things are good and will help all people.* Titus 3:4-5, 8 (ICB)

"But I just want to be a 'Pew Tater,'" you may say. "Isn't it enough that I attend and tithe?"

Suiting up and showing up is a good start, but the apostles told us a relationship with Christ involves more. James, the half-brother of Jesus, offered: *But don't just listen to God's word. You must do what it says. Otherwise, you are only fooling yourselves.* James 1:22 (NLT).

If anyone, then, knows the good they ought to do and doesn't do it, it is sin for them. James 4:17 (NIV)

Paul put emphasis on good works. *Tell them to use their money to do good. They should be rich in good works and generous to those in need, always being ready to share with others.* 1 Timothy 6:18 (NLT)

Granted, not everyone is called to serve as a missionary in Zimbabwe or to spend their days feeding the poor, but we all have been given talents that can be used to serve the Lord.

We were involved in a discussion with our friends in an assisted living facility about the kind of things the elderly can do for others. One dear lady in her 90s knits prayer shawls. Another mentioned that she helps those with limited sight play bingo, while another mentioned filling gift boxes for our troops. Others talked about the power of a gentle touch, a kind word, a friendly smile, or a quiet prayer. Sometimes the most valuable thing we can offer the Lord is our time helping others.

John Wesley encouraged us: "Do all the good you can, by all the means you can, in all the ways you can, in all the places you can, at all the times you can, to all the people you can, as long as ever you can."

In Matthew 25, we learn goodness involves reaching out to all of God's children. *"And the King will answer and say to them, 'Assuredly, I say to you, inasmuch as you did it to one of the least of these My brethren, you did it to Me.'"* Matthew 25:40 (NKJV)

Does it matter when we do good? Without a doubt! Everything we do that brings glory to God matters.

> *May the favor of the Lord our God rest on us; establish the work of our hands for us—yes, establish the work of our hands.*
>
> PSALM 90:17 (NIV)

WHO'LL MOVE THE CHAIRS?

The satellite church had moved into its new location. The first week, a team of eight volunteers packed chairs, tables, and audio-visual equipment into a 20-foot trailer and moved it from the main campus to the satellite location. At the end of the service, the team packed everything back into the trailer and returned it to the main campus. All totaled, the team spent about eight hours making sure everything was taken care of. By the third week, the team had dropped from eight to six members. By the fourth week, it was a team of four.

Moving chairs can be back-breaking work. Chairs are heavier than they look, so arranging the seating for one hundred worshippers is not a job for "light-weights." The team of four, it turned out, was not made up of men you'd expect to see doing heavy-lifting. One was seventy-five; one was sixty-two, the other two were younger, but not so young as to make the chair detail a walk in the park, so it was not an unreasonable request when the team leader asked several men who were standing by if they would be willing to help. His request prompted a cascade of excuses.

"I have to check on my kids in the nursery." one explained.

Another responded, "I was planning to meet with the pastor."

"I'm heading up a small group" was the response of one young man whose small group would be starting the following month.

The man who shared this story with me was one of the four remaining members of the chair-moving team. He was frustrated, hurt, and ready to not only quit the team but to change churches.

Jesus said, *"The harvest is great, but the workers are few. So pray to the Lord who is in charge of the harvest; ask him to send more workers into his fields.* Luke 10:2b (NLT)

Do you have gifts you can use as a worker in the harvest field? Perhaps, you have the gift of helping.

God has placed in the church first of all apostles, second prophets, third teachers, then miracles, then gifts of healing, of helping, of guidance, and of different kinds of tongues. 1 Corinthians 12:28 (NIV)

The men who stood by while the team of four handled the set-up probably didn't realize they do indeed have the gift of chair-moving and the gift of picking up trash or packing boxes. It's called the gift of helping. Picking up bulletins or replacing hymnals in their holders is another form of helping, of serving, and serving is a form of worship.

Each of you should use whatever gift you have received to serve others, as faithful stewards of God's grace in its various forms. 1 Peter 4:10

All of us can serve. Maybe your talents are in the area of encouraging; you can offer a hug or a comforting word to someone who is hurting. Maybe your gift is hospitality; you can be a greeter, or simply take the time to welcome someone who is new to your church.

Take counsel from 1st Corinthians: *There are different kinds of gifts, but the same Spirit distributes them. There are different kinds of service, but the same Lord. There are different kinds of working, but in all of them and in everyone it is the same God at work.* 1 Corinthians 12:4-6

A pastor with a good message can make members and visitors happy they came, but it's often the members in the chairs (chairs that someone put in place) who make them want to come back.

CONFLICT IN GOD'S FAMILY

Now I appeal to Euodia and Syntyche. Please, because you belong to the Lord, settle your disagreement. And I ask you, my true partner, to help these two women, for they worked hard with me in telling others the Good News. They worked along with Clement and the rest of my co-workers, whose names are written in the Book of Life. Philippians 4:2-3 (NLT)

Imagine that! Church members who are in conflict. We don't know the issues that led Eurodia and Syntyche to be at odds, but we know the conflict was serious enough for the apostle Paul to address it in his letter to the church of Philippi. In verses four and five, Paul tied joy in the Lord to our treating others gently.

Rejoice in the Lord always. I will say it again: Rejoice! Let your gentleness be evident to all. The Lord is near. Philippians 4:4-5 (NIV)

Over my seventy-four plus years, I have been a church-hopper, attending churches of many denominations: Episcopal, Baptist, Methodist, Foursquare Gospel, Church of God, Catholic, Greek Orthodox, Presbyterian, Lutheran, Community Bible, Calvary Chapel, and mega-churches such as Mariners and Saddleback. One thing all churches must deal with is conflict. Conflict can rob brothers and sisters in Christ of their joy in the Lord.

What causes this conflict? Pride, jealousy, judgementalism, and fear are common triggers; all of which have to do with how we measure our self-worth. We have egos, and when we let other people define us, or we attempt to define others, we Edge God Out.

God sees each of his children as a new creation, as righteous and set apart, as forgiven and loved. When we start to see ourselves and see others as God sees us, we are on the path to reclaiming the joy we may have lost.

Verses that tell us how God sees us:

As his children: *But to all who believed him and accepted him, he gave the right to become children of God.* John 1:12 (NLT)

As a new creation: *Therefore, if anyone is in Christ, he is a new creation; old things have passed away; behold, all things have become new."* 2 Cor. 5:17 (NKJV)

As righteous and holy: *Put on your new nature, created to be like God–truly righteous and holy.* Ephesians 4:24 (NLT)

As forgiven: *I am writing to you, dear children, because your sins have been forgiven on account of his name.* 1 John 2:12 (NIV)

As his beloved: *And this hope will not lead to disappointment. For we know how dearly God loves us, because he has given us the Holy Spirit to fill our hearts with his love.* Romans 5:5 (NLT)

What can we do when we find ourselves in conflict with a brother or sister in Christ?

A starting point might be to see how our ego may be involved. If we discover we are prideful, we can reflect on the words in Philippians: *Do nothing out of selfish ambition or vain conceit. Rather, in humility value others above yourselves, not looking to your own interests but each of you to the interests of the others.* Philippians 2:3-4 (NIV)

Perhaps we are jealous. The antidote to jealousy is thankfulness. *Let the peace of Christ rule in your hearts, since as members of one body you were called to peace. And be thankful.* Colossians 3:15

Are we judgmental? *Be kind and compassionate to one another, forgiving each other, just as in Christ God forgave you.* Ephesians 4:32

Fear can also trigger conflict in a relationship. We need to learn to put our trust in the One who can calm our fears and heal our relationships. *Fear of man will prove to be a snare, but whoever trusts in the Lord is kept safe.* Proverbs 29:25

Once we confront the part "our" ego may be playing in the conflict, we can take a strong step toward reconciliation by praying for the other person.

And pray in the Spirit on all occasions with all kinds of prayers and requests. With this in mind, be alert and always keep on praying for all the Lord's people. Ephesians 6:18

Not sure what to pray? For twenty-one days, pray for the person you resent to have something you want for yourself. For instance, pray the Holy Spirit will produce in each of you the fruit of *love, joy, peace, forbearance, kindness, goodness, faithfulness, gentleness and self-control.* Galatians 5:22-23b These are, after all, qualities that will help you keep from pulling the triggers of conflict.

"The Fog"

There's a fog that clouds our vision.
Fog obscures the goal.
In Christ that fog is lifted;
the broken are made whole.
Christ can join the pieces.
He helps the parts unite.
He fits them all together;
they're perfect in his sight.
That fog is of our making
In God's eyes, we are one.
And when we are united
the fog's cleared by the Son.

I appeal to you, brothers and sisters, in the name of our Lord
Jesus Christ, that all of you agree with one another in what
you say and that there be no divisions among you, but that
you be perfectly united in mind and thought.

1 CORINTHIANS 1:10 (NIV)

LIKE YOU WANT THEM TO GO TO HEAVEN

This righteousness of God comes through faith in Jesus Christ for all
those [Jew or Gentile] who believe [and trust in Him and acknowledge
Him as God's Son]. There is no distinction, since all have sinned and
continually fall short of the glory of God, Romans 3:22-23 (AMP)

Have you ever heard a sermon that targeted one of your weaknesses so directly you almost wished you had stayed home that week? I'm thinking about the kind of sermon that identifies an area where your repentance is required, but where you may not yet be ready or willing to make necessary changes.

One Sunday, Pastor Mike Johnson from Grace Hills Church in Laguna Niguel gave a sermon entitled "Living Right." Mike used the first seven verses from the book of Titus to develop a list of guidelines for living a Christian lifestyle. One of Pastor Mike's sermon points became a scale I can now use to measure just how far I still must go. He said, "Don't forget to treat everybody like you want them to go to heaven."

Really? Who is everybody, anyway? We can get in the habit of caring about and praying only for those we approve of, while those we disapprove of may be the ones most in need of our prayers. Imagine how our attitudes might change, how much stronger our Christian walk might get, if we adopted a "heaven for everyone" approach. Wouldn't we be more patient, kinder, more eager to share the gospel?

When I asked Bonnie what it would mean if she treated everyone like she wanted them to go to heaven, she said, "It would mean my love for them would be greater than my self-righteous indignation."

A few days later she had the opportunity to put this thought to the test. One of her acquaintances made a comment Bonnie found to be quite insensitive. Bonnie was hurt and ready to give her friend a sharp retort when she remembered the sermon. Instead of responding with a sarcastic or cutting remark, she simply walked away. "Sometimes silence can be a form of prayer." She told me.

A few days later, the friend called to thank her for the lunch they had shared and to tell her how much Bonnie's prayers meant to her. Her friend then told her she would soon be going into the hospital for tests. A condition the doctors had told her was not serious, now, it appeared, might be cancer.

Talking about the incident, Bonnie reflected, "Just think how devastated both of us would have been had I said something that damaged our friendship."

Of course, there will be times when treating someone like we want them to go to heaven might seem impossible. We just don't like some people; that's human nature, so we may have to, as Pastor Mike's wife suggested, treat them like we want them to go to heaven . . . just in a different mansion.

The other mansion?

Just kidding. I'm sure the pastor's wife had something better for them in mind.

With others, their offense may be so egregious, our pain so great, or our faith too small for us to love them enough to even wish them well. We may not believe they deserve to go to heaven.

Another point from Pastor Mike's sermon helped me get past my self-righteous assessment of who might be "worthy" for heaven: His point: "Don't forget people haven't always thought you were going to heaven."

> For it is by grace [God's remarkable compassion and favor drawing you to Christ] that you have been saved [actually delivered from judgment and given eternal life] through faith. And this [salvation] is not of yourselves [not through your own effort], but it is the [undeserved, gracious] gift of God.

EPHESIANS 2:8

THE GOSSIP'S PLAN

I made a plan to never say a thing that isn't true,
to never talk in whispered breath about a friend like you,
to never ever gossip or lend an eager ear.
My plan is not to gossip; I think I'll start next year!

When I was nine or ten years old, I ran up to my mother and whispered into her ear something I had heard about a neighbor. She gave me one of those looks only a mother can give, then said softly, "Whispering is lying; lying's a sin. If you ever get to heaven, you'll never get in." Mom, like most of us, knew how easy it is to slip into the sin of gossip.

Just how serious is gossip? The flippant answer might be, "Depends on whether you are the "gossiper" or the "gossipee," but the Bible doesn't see gossip as a minor infraction.

Psalm 39:1 puts it this way: *I said, "I will be careful how I act. I will not sin by what I say. I will be careful what I say around wicked people."*

Need a picture of a gossip? Check out Psalm 64:3-4: *They sharpen their tongues like swords. They shoot bitter words like arrows. They hide and shoot at innocent people. They shoot suddenly and are not afraid.*

Anyone who has been the victim of gossip may feel like the psalmist who wrote, *When I was in trouble, I called to the Lord. And he answered me. Lord, save me from liars and from those who plan evil.* Psalm 120:1-2

Proverbs 11:12-13 reads, *A person without good sense finds fault with his neighbor. But a person with understanding keeps quiet. A person who gossips can't keep secrets. But a trustworthy person can keep a secret.*

Proverbs 17:4 makes it clear that listening to gossip is on a level with speaking gossip. *An evil person listens to evil words. A liar pays attention to cruel words.*

Proverbs 20:19 offers advice: *Gossips can't keep secrets. So avoid people who talk too much.*

In the book of Romans, gossips are grouped with slanderers, God-haters, the insolent, those who are arrogant and the boastful. The apostle Paul also wrote of his concerns about the Church at Corinth, *I am afraid that among you there may be arguing, jealousy, anger, selfish fighting, evil talk, gossip, pride, and confusion.* 2 Corinthians 12:20b

The apostle James wrote a searing indictment of gossip: *A person might think he is religious. But if he says things he should not say, then he is just fooling himself. His "religion" is worth nothing."* James 1:26

And the apostle Peter offered his "Amen" when he wrote, *A person must do these things to enjoy life and have many, happy days. He must not say evil things. He must not tell lies.* 1 Peter 3:10

Turning again to the book of James, we see the emphasis the apostle put on controlling the tongue. *We all make many mistakes. If there were a person who never said anything wrong, he would be perfect. He would be able to control his whole body, too.* James 3:2

When you are tempted to gossip, try this simple rule: Don't say anything in a whisper that you wouldn't be willing to shout from the rooftop.

The apostle James explains *People can tame every kind of wild animal, bird, reptile, and fish, and they have tamed them. But no one can tame the tongue. It is wild and evil. It is full of poison that can kill.* James 3:7-8

All the scriptures in this particular devotion came from the *International Children's Bible.* After all, the message is one we've been hearing since we were kids, "If you can't say something nice about someone, don't say anything at all."

Lord, who may enter your Holy Tent? Who may live on your holy mountain? Only a person who is innocent and who does what is right. He must speak the truth from his heart. He must not tell lies about others. He must do no wrong to his neighbors. He must not gossip.

PSALM 15:1-3

IS EVERYBODY WELCOME?

My childhood church was The Church of the Epiphany, located a few blocks from the White House in downtown Washington, D.C. This was a very "proper" church, where gentlemen wore ties, and most ladies wore hats. Decorative nails on the pews prompted ushers to reserve seats for larger donors. As a young man, I'm pretty sure I never heard a sermon at Epiphany based on the words of the Scripture below.

My dear brothers and sisters, how can you claim to have faith in our glorious Lord Jesus Christ if you favor some people over others? For example, suppose someone comes into your meeting dressed in fancy clothes and expensive jewelry, and another comes in who is poor and dressed in dirty clothes. If you give special attention and a good seat to the rich person, but you say to the poor one, "You can stand over there, or else sit on the floor"—well, doesn't this discrimination show that your judgments are guided by evil motives?

Listen to me, dear brothers and sisters. Hasn't God chosen the poor in this world to be rich in faith? Aren't they the ones who will inherit the Kingdom he promised to those who love him? James 2:1-5 (NLT)

Miriam-Webster.com defines epiphany: "a moment in which you suddenly see or understand something in a new or very clear way." A couple of years ago, I had my own epiphany when I had the opportunity to once again attend a church service at the Church of the Epiphany. The pews still had the decorative nails, but now, homeless men and women slept where the elite had once worshipped. No one seemed to take notice of the poor who had taken refuge in the church, except when one of the ladies of the church would shake one of the sleepers who had started to snore a bit too loudly. All are welcome.

In Matthew 11:28, Jesus said, *"Come to me, all of you who are weary and carry heavy burdens, and I will give you rest."* He didn't impose a dress code; he offered his rest to all who would come to him. Are we as welcoming as Jesus? Are we willing to embrace all who need the Lord or just those that fit into our comfort zone?

A while back, I went for my regular haircut at John's Barber Lounge in Lake Forest. A gray-haired white guy is a bit out of place at John's. I don't ask for a fade with texture. The only gang I ever belonged to is the Marine Corps, and tattoos just aren't my thing. But since I get a good haircut and it's cheap, John's Barber Lounge is where I go.

As I sat down in the chair, Philly, a former drug user whose looks reflect his rough past asked, "Aren't you the dude who dropped off that worship tape for one of the barbers?"

"Yes. I thought she might need it."

With a loving look he said, "Bro, she needs that and a lot more!" He shook his head, and spent the next ten minutes sharing with me how someone had brought him to Christ and changed his life—someone who was not concerned by what he *looked* like, but with what he could *be* like.

Lord, help us to see people as you see them and to share your love wherever we can.

"Heaven's Fashion Show"

Last night I had a crazy dream; what caused it I don't know.
It might have been the sauerkraut or my last cup of "Joe."
I tossed and turned; I tried to sleep; My wife gave me a nudge.
I dreamed of heaven's fashion show, and I became a judge.
The runway wasn't paved with gold, and there was no applause.
The models weren't what you'd expect, in fact, they made me pause.
None were wearing fancy clothes from Gucci, Coach or Chu.
It seemed the very best of them was dressed much worse than you.
In dungarees, in funny hats, in shoes worn thin from use,
was this a freakish fashion show or just runway abuse?
Abuse of all the rules I'd known of proper ways to dress?
This couldn't be a fashion show; this was a fashion mess!
Just then, the Chief Judge took his place and told me to depart.
"You judge a person's outer self; I look upon the heart.
My temple is a holy place and it deserves respect,
but judging folks for how they look is not what I expect.
I love the flashy fashion plate whose clothes mask inner fears.
I love the man in cutoff jeans who's served the poor for years.
I even love the pastor whom some people criticize;
her humble clothes conceal a heart that's precious in my eyes."
I woke to find it was a dream, and boy, was I relieved.
I thanked the Lord and took to heart the warning I'd received.
I pray the Chief Judge, Jesus Christ, will help me do my part
to share his love by looking for the good that's in the heart.

"The Lord doesn't see things the way you see them. People
judge by outward appearance, but the Lord looks at the heart."

1 SAMUEL 16:7B (NLT)

ROOF-RIPPIN' RELATIONSHIPS

Imagine sitting in a Bible study. The teacher is offering a spellbinding explanation of a section of Scripture when suddenly you notice material falling from the ceiling. A small hole opens, then gets larger until you see several men peering down at you through the hole. The hole gets even larger and you see a man being lowered on a mat. What do you think would be going through your mind?

Perhaps you would just wonder what those guys are up to. Maybe you'd be upset that your study was being interrupted. If you were the homeowner, you might rightly ask, "Who's gonna repair my roof?

> *A few days later, when Jesus again entered Capernaum, the people heard that he had come home. They gathered in such large numbers that there was no room left, not even outside the door, and he preached the word to them. Some men came, bringing to him a paralyzed man, carried by four of them. Since they could not get him to Jesus because of the crowd, they made an opening in the roof above Jesus by digging through it and then lowered the mat the man was lying on. When Jesus saw their faith, he said to the paralyzed man, "Son, your sins are forgiven." Mark 2:1-5 (NIV)*

The four men in the above story from Mark didn't really give any thought to the consequences of their actions. They had a "roof-ripping" relationship which motivated them to do whatever was required to help their friend.

I was discussing this Scripture with my friend Rand. He offered a question we might want to think about: "Who would be the four friends who would take such an extreme measure to help you?"

A related question would be, "Whom would you be willing to rip through a roof to help?"

That leads to a third question: Just how far, as Christians, must we go to live Jesus' command to "*Do to others as you would have them do unto you.*" Luke 6:31?

In this Scripture, Jesus sets a high bar when it comes to loving the unloved. The bar must be even higher when it comes to how we relate to brothers and sisters in Christ.

We find a formula for Christian relationships in Colossians, which reads in part:

> *Therefore, as God's chosen people, holy and dearly loved, clothe yourselves with compassion, kindness, humility, gentleness and patience. Bear with each other and forgive one another if any of you has a grievance against someone. Forgive as the Lord forgave you. And over all these virtues put on love, which binds them all together in perfect unity.*
>
> *Let the peace of Christ rule in your hearts, since as members of one body you were called to peace. And be thankful . . . And whatever you do, whether in word or deed, do it all in the name of the Lord Jesus, giving thanks to God the Father through him.* Colossians 3:12-15,17

There will be times when friends want you to tear through a metaphorical roof for them, but all you are capable of is praying the Lord will send someone who is better able to help them. There will be other times when their demands are unreasonable or cross boundaries where your only response can be an unequivocal "no."

Then, there are the times when you'll want to "tear the house down" for someone when all they really need is for you to understand the chaos in which they live. Whatever the situation, the best first step is to be still and pray that God, acting through the Holy Spirit, will lead you to know and to do His will.

In Proverbs 18:24b we read, *there is a friend who sticks closer than a brother.* This kind of friendship is a special gift from God, and if you have such a friend, you should cherish him or her. Our prayer would be that God would help each of us to have, and to be that kind of friend.

Let us not become weary in doing good, for at the proper time we will reap a harvest if we donot give up.

GALATIANS 6:9

THE FLOODGATES OF HEAVEN

One of my pet peeves is pastors who use guilt to pressure their flock to give more, serve more, or whatever. Don't take me wrong; I believe in and practice biblical tithing. I also encourage donating to worthy charities and recognize that service to our brothers and sisters in Christ can be a fulfilling endeavor. My problem is with the guilt-based appeals some use to promote tithing.

For many churches, autumn is the time for stewardship campaigns. I have attended churches where the stewardship campaign feels more like a "shakedown" than an opportunity to share in the development of God's Kingdom. Rather than being presented as an offering of thanks to God, that shows we put Him first in our lives, the tithe is treated like a past due I.O.U.

One weekend, for instance, Bonnie and I decided to attend a church we had attended about seven years ago. When the pastor gave a sermon in which he proclaimed, "The reason many people don't tithe is that they are greedy," we remembered one of the reasons we had left that church in the first place.

Miriam-Webster defines stewardship as "the careful and responsible management of something entrusted to one's care." As children of God, we are called to carefully manage the resources

God has provided each of us. Part of this management involves supporting the place we worship. But using guilt or shame to meet stewardship goals is manipulative and an insult to God's grace.

The apostle Paul offered this guidance: *Each of you should give what you have decided in your heart to give, not reluctantly or under compulsion, for God loves a cheerful giver.* 2 Corinthians 9:7 (NIV)

For many, tithing is the "third rail" in religion. There was a time in my life when I would pretty much skip out on church services from late October to early December because I knew they'd be asking for money. But my attitude toward tithing started to change when I took the challenge in Malachi 3:10 and decided to test God by getting serious about tithing.

Bring the whole tithe into the storehouse, that there may be food in my house. Test me in this," says the LORD Almighty, "and see if I will not throw open the floodgates of heaven and pour out so much blessing that there will not be room enough to store it. Malachi 3:10

An amazing thing happened. I stopped worrying about scarcity and discovered a new abundance in God. The floodgates of heaven truly do pour out blessings we can hardly imagine.

I no longer skip out on services during the stewardship season. Pastors, including my own, still drive me up the wall when they try to guilt me into giving more, but I try to remember I'm not giving to them. I'm giving to God through them and pray they will use my gifts for God's glory.

You will be enriched in every way so that you can be generous on every occasion, and through us your generosity will result in thanksgiving to God.

2 CORINTHIANS 9:11

THE DEVIL IS REAL

Some may accuse you of being paranoid about Satan,
but it's not paranoia when someone really is out to get you.

BE ALERT AND OF SOBER MIND.
YOUR ENEMY THE DEVIL PROWLS AROUND LIKE A
ROARING LION LOOKING FOR SOMEONE TO DEVOUR.

1 Peter 5:8 (NIV)

THE DEVIL'S BAIT SHOP

When we talk about the devil, we're not talking about that fictional character with a red satin suit, neatly trimmed Van Dyke style beard and horns. We are talking about Satan, the accuser, the deceiver, the adversary. We are warned about him. *Stay alert! Watch out for your great enemy, the devil. He prowls around like a roaring lion, looking for someone to devour.* 1 Peter 5:8 (NLT)

The Message Bible offers the following ending for the Lord's Prayer: *"Keep us safe from ourselves and the Devil."* Luke 11:4b (MSG)

The apostle Paul tells us, *Put on all of God's armor so that you will be able to stand firm against all strategies of the devil.* Ephesians 6:11 (NLT)

In James 4:7, James, the half-brother of Jesus wrote, *So humble yourselves before God. Resist the devil, and he will flee from you.*

The devil will do everything he can to tempt us; we don't have to take the bait!

"The Devil's Bait Shop"
An original poem inspired by *The Bait of Satan* by John Bevere

The devil crossed his arms and smiled with delight.
He didn't need to interfere; he'd simply let them fight.
He'd let them tear each other down; he'd let them castigate.
No need for him to stoke the fire; he merely had to wait.
Oh! He might whisper in her ear to kindle thoughts of shame
or give a nudge to those who judge to show them who to blame.
The devil uses each of us to spread his deadly bait;
with unkind words or selfish deeds, we seal another's fate.
So, watch the words you're casting, and watch which hooks you take;
reflect, instead, the love of Christ with every choice you make.
And pray the Holy Spirit will guide you through life's maze.
Avoid the Devil's bait shop. Let Jesus' name be praised.

Above all, clothe yourselves with love, which binds us all to-gether in perfect harmony. And let the peace that comes from Christ rule in your hearts. For as members of one body you are called to live in peace. And always be thankful.

COLOSSIANS 3:14-15

AVOIDING THE ROCKS

I once worked for Imperial Manufacturing Company, the firm that developed the offshore survival suit. If you have watched the TV show, "The Deadliest Catch," you may have seen the fishermen wearing the large, red, full-body suit that allows them to survive for several hours in frigid arctic waters.

One weekend, Nick, the company president and I became actors, as we shot a video of the suits in use. We donned our survival suits and jumped from a Coast Guard rescue boat into the choppy waters off Astoria, Washington. The tide changes near the mouth of the Columbia River make for some of the most dangerous water in the world. We knew it would be the perfect place to make our video.

Everything was going according to plan until suddenly the tide started to change. Floating on my back in the huge neoprene suit, I was unaware of any danger until I heard the low clanging of a bell – ding, swish, ding, swish.

Nick was within a few yards of me, so I shouted to ask him what the bell was. He paddled hard to change his position, then shouted back to me, "Don, we are in trouble. That's a channel buoy—we're being swept onto the rocks."

I started paddling like crazy and managed to get back into the current. Good news, bad news, we were now being swept out to sea. The Coast Guard rescue boat made a couple of attempts to pick us up, but as the waves became rougher, the decision was made to call for a helicopter rescue.

You can't begin to imagine how relieved I was when we were finally lifted into the hatch of the helicopter in a rescue sling. My guardian angel had rotor blades, not wings!

I share this story because it provides an interesting metaphor for how people handle their sin. The Bible tells us the wages of sin is death. But, just like the waters off Astoria, sin may initially seem like something we can handle. The problem is that the sea of sin is unpredictable. The changing tide pulled me toward the rocks. Similarly, sin has its own magnetic pull. A small taste of sin whets the appetite for more. We indulge until our lives are slowly pulled out of control.

Sin pulls us away from relationships with friends, away from relationships with family, and most damaging, away from our relationship with God.

"But I'm a Christian," you may say. "I am washed by Jesus' blood. All that I have to do is confess my sins and all is forgiven." Satan loves for you to fall for that lie.

The apostle Paul gives us the response: *What shall we say, then? Shall we go on sinning so that grace may increase? By no means! We are those who have died to sin; how can we live in it any longer?* Romans 6:1-2 (NIV)

Satan wants us to keep on sinning. God wants us to repent and turn to Him. Repentance involves four distinct actions:

- Admitting or confessing sin.
- Ceasing the sin
- Resolving to not repeat the offense.
- Making restitution or amends where possible.

If all we do is confess our sin, we may have encountered the warning buoy, but we are still headed for the rocks. There is a huge difference between a confession that comes from a broken spirit and a flippant confession without repentance, "My bad! You caught me!"

In 2nd Corinthians 7:10, we read, *Godly sorrow brings repentance that leads to salvation and leaves no regret, but worldly sorrow brings death.*

To confess and then go on sinning is to be caught in a current that may ultimately lead to disaster. The good news is that just like there was a helicopter standing by to pull me from the threatening waters, there is a Savior who wants to give us a lifeline, and we all need to do is repent and turn to him.

We can take comfort in Jesus' words, *"There will be more rejoicing in heaven over one sinner who repents than over ninety-nine righteous persons who do not need to repent."* LUKE 15:7B

"Coud it Be?"

Could it be that God expected too much
when he formed that lump of clay?

Did He know the path we'd choose to take,
that we'd choose to walk away?

Did He know His love would be cast aside
as self-love took His place?

Could it be God that expected too much
when He made the human race?

Could it be that we expected too much
when we found that life was tough?

Could it be we turned too quickly to self,
crying, "God is not enough?"

Did we pull Him down from his heavenly realm
and make Him a fallible man?

Or did He decide to come down on his own
as part of a wonderful plan?

Could it be that Jesus expected too much as he
hung on a tree of shame?

When he felt abandoned and cried to the Father,
did God even stop to explain?

Could it be that Jesus had known all along
he'd be sent as an innocent lamb

To give us a way to come back to God's love?
Are you ready to come? I am.

But he was pierced for our rebellion, crushed for our sins.
He was beaten so we could be whole.
He was whipped so we could be healed.
All of us, like sheep, have strayed away.
We have left God's paths to follow our own.
Yet the Lord laid on him the sins of us all.

ISAIAH 53:5-6 (NLT)

JESUS IN THE WILDERNESS

Knowing Bonnie and I had visited Israel, Christina, a dear friend recommended we read *Jesus: A Pilgrimage*. In this book, James Martin, S.J., a Jesuit priest, chronicles his visit to the holy land. As he writes about each stop on his pilgrimage, the author does a wonderful job of transporting the reader back to 1st century Palestine.

Father Martin uses readings from the Scriptures plus historical and archeological data to give the reader an understanding of what conditions were like in Jesus' day. He retraces Christ's life as presented in the Gospels and highlights the human side of Jesus that is often overlooked.

This book motivated Bonnie and me to look more closely at sections of Scripture we may have previously skimmed over. When we read to discover Jesus the man, we find a person who faced many of the issues we struggle with. He was hungry and thirsty. He got tired. He had problems with his siblings. He had friends and he had enemies. He, too, faced temptation.

Then Jesus was led by the Spirit into the wilderness to be tempted there by the devil. For forty days and forty nights he fasted and became very hungry. Matthew 4:1-2 (NLT)

What is the significance of Jesus' temptation? Father Martin saw it as preparation for the ministry Jesus was about to embark upon. "Jesus was free from sin, but not temptation." In his moments with

Satan, Martin explains, "He aligned himself with sinful humanity." That is, he put himself in a position where he felt what we feel.

The three temptations Satan used with Jesus are prototypical of temptations we face.

First, Satan tempted Jesus to satisfy his physical needs. *"If you are the Son of God, tell these stones to become loaves of bread."* Matthew 4:3b When we are hungry or tired or dissatisfied with our current conditions, Satan can use our needs to tempt us to want even more.

Then, Satan tempted Jesus by challenging his identity. *"If you are the Son of God, jump off!* [the highest point in the temple]*!"* Matthew 4:6b—Whenever we feel the need to get our sense of worth from others, we open another door to Satan.

And then, Satan used the promise of position and power. *Next the devil took him to the peak of a very high mountain and showed him all the kingdoms of the world and their glory. "I will give it all to you,"* he said, *"if you will kneel down and worship me."* Matthew 4:8-9

When we put anything in our lives above God, Satan offers us a pathway to destruction. Jesus rebuffed each of Satan's attempts and gave us a defense we can turn to when we are tempted. *"Get out of here, Satan," Jesus told him. "For the Scriptures say, 'You must worship the Lord your God and serve only him."* Matthew 4:10

"Jesus," Father Martin offers, "was not play-acting at being human." He faced temptation just as we face temptation, but unlike us, Jesus proved to be blameless. "God fashioned him into just the instrument God needed for the salvation of the world."

God made him who had no sin to be sin for us, so that in him we might become the righteousness of God. 2 Corinthians 5:21 (NIV)

When we meditate on the story of Jesus' temptation in the wilderness, the words in the Lord's Prayer: *"Lead us not into temptation, but deliver us from evil"* become even more powerful for us. Jesus didn't just say them, he lived them.

And this is my prayer: that your love may abound more and more in knowledge and depth of insight, so that you may be able to discern what is best and may be pure and blameless for the day of Christ, filled with the fruit of righteousness that comes through Jesus Christ—to the glory and praise of God.

PHILIPPIANS 1:9-11

HELP ME IN MY UNBELIEF

One morning, I was waiting for the bus when a young man standing near me suddenly started convulsing violently. He fell to the ground and started foaming at the mouth. I knelt beside him and tried to hold him steady.

A young woman dressed in a white uniform approached, so remembering something I had been taught in a first-aid class, I shouted, "He's having a seizure. You can use my comb to keep him from swallowing his tongue." (This was in the 1960s; this procedure is no longer recommended.)

She had a horrified look on her face as she wrapped the comb in a handkerchief, placed it in the victim's mouth and held it there until he calmed. Fortunately, we were close to a hospital and an emergency unit soon appeared. After the ambulance left, I went over to thank the nurse for her help. "I can't tell you how thankful I was to see your nurse's uniform," I said.

Still visibly shaken the young lady replied, "Nurse? Nurse? I'm a waitress!"

I wonder if Jesus' disciples felt somewhat like my waitress felt when they encountered a boy who suffered from convulsions. The story is found in the ninth chapter of Mark.

Jesus came upon a crowd where some of his disciples were arguing with teachers of the law.

"What are you arguing with them about?" he asked.

A man in the crowd answered, "Teacher, I brought you my son, who is possessed by a spirit that has robbed him of speech. Whenever it seizes him, it throws him to the ground. He foams at the mouth, gnashes his teeth and becomes rigid. I asked your disciples to drive out the spirit, but they could not."

"O unbelieving generation," Jesus replied, "how long shall I stay with you? How long shall I put up with you? Bring the boy to me."

So they brought him. When the spirit saw Jesus, it immediately threw the boy into a convulsion. He fell to the ground and rolled around, foaming at the mouth. Jesus asked the boy's father, "How long has he been like this?"

"From childhood," he answered. "It has often thrown him into fire or water to kill him. But if you can do anything, take pity on us and help us."

"'If you can'?" said Jesus. "Everything is possible for him who believes."

Immediately the boy's father exclaimed, "I do believe; help me overcome my unbelief!"

When Jesus saw that a crowd was running to the scene, he rebuked the evil spirit. "You deaf and mute spirit," he said, "I command you, come out of him and never enter him again."

The spirit shrieked, convulsed him violently and came out. The boy looked so much like a corpse that many said, "He's dead." But Jesus took him by the hand and lifted him to his feet, and he stood up.

After Jesus had gone indoors, his disciples asked him privately, "Why couldn't we drive it out?"

He replied, "This kind can come out only by prayer."

Mark 9:16-29 (NIV)

In this story, Jesus' disciples realized their powerlessness. They had fallen into the all-too- human trap of believing "they" had the power. They failed because they forgot all power comes from God. None of them, it seems, had asked the question, "Should we pray about this?"

Now, let's turn our attention from the disciples to the father in the story. It is likely he had heard of the miracles Jesus had been performing. He wanted to believe but wasn't sure Jesus would be any more capable of curing his son than the disciples, who had already failed. His response to Jesus, "*I do believe. Help me overcome my unbelief.*" is one of the most honest expressions of faith in the Bible.

The Greek word *apistia* which is translated in this Scripture as "unbelief" can also be translated, "want of trust and confidence." We have been taught "*With God all things are possible,*" but like the father in the story, we may not have rock-solid confidence that a specific prayer will be answered. The reality is God may say, "Yes." He may say, "No," or He might say, "Wait."

It is normal to have doubts. It's how we respond to our doubts that makes the difference. Examining our doubts can strengthen our faith; ignoring them may ultimately undermine our faith. Even Jesus' disciples had doubts, some of which were not resolved until after Jesus' resurrection.

The story about the boy possessed by demons is also found in the book of Matthew. Look at this translation from the International Children's Bible.

Jesus answered, "You were not able to drive out the demon because your faith is too small. I tell you the truth. If your faith is as big as a mustard seed, you can say to this mountain, 'Move from here to there.'

And the mountain will move. All things will be possible for you. Matthew 17:20 (ICB)

I don't believe Jesus used the example of the mustard seed to say that a small amount of faith is all that is needed. Rather, his message may be that faith must be a living, growing thing. Seeds need to be planted, watered, and nourished; so must faith.

You pray, and God says, "Yes." Your faith grows.

You pray, and God says, "No." Seek to understand God's will for your life.

You pray, and God says, "Wait." Remember, only He knows the future.

> *Mountains aren't moved in a moment. As faith grows, our personal "mountains" seem smaller and more conquerable. Our dream is to reach the level of faith where we, like the apostle Paul can say, I can do all thing's through Christ who strengthens me.*

PHILIPPIANS 4:13 (NKJV)

WE WANT TO DO GOOD,
BUT WE DON'T

AND I KNOW THAT NOTHING GOOD LIVES IN ME,
THAT IS, IN MY SINFUL NATURE.
I WANT TO DO WHAT IS RIGHT, BUT I CAN'T.
I WANT TO DO WHAT IS GOOD, BUT I DON'T.
I DON'T WANT TO DO WHAT IS
WRONG, BUT I DO IT ANYWAY.

Romans 7:18-19 (NLT)

"Heading for Sin's Falls"

You're floating down a river when from the bank Christ calls,
"Come join me on the shore, child; you're heading for the falls."
Flowing with the rapids, you surge toward your goal,
ignoring rocks and current, the peril to your soul.
It may be the excitement, the need to feel the rush,
or maybe you feel fearless; it's your own strength you trust.
But strength someday will vanish, and thrills will seem a waste
when fearless thoughts are absent, and terror takes their place.
Avoid Sin's Falls by listening to Jesus' calming voice.
"Come join me on the shore, child. It really is your choice."

*When you go through deep waters and great trouble, I will
be with you. When you go through rivers of difficulty, you
will not drown!*

ISAIAH 43:2A (TLB)

HOW MANY DIMPLES ON A GOLF BALL?

Being a golfer, I was interested in learning how many dimples are on a regulation golf ball. I discovered, "You can get between 300 and 500 dimples on quality golf balls. However, for regulation golf balls, 336 dimples is a common number." (wetalkaboutgolf.com)

Next question: How many commandments are there? Two? Ten? Six-hundred thirteen?

Jewish tradition holds there are 613 commandments (Mitavot) in the Torah. The most widely accepted listing was compiled by the Rabbi Moshe ben Maimon, one of the greatest medieval Jewish scholars. Better known to the secular world as Maimonides. You can see one compilation of these commandments at http://www.jewfaq.org/613.htm.

Christians are more familiar with the Ten Commandments as found in Exodus 20:2-17 (NLT)

> "I am the Lord your God, who rescued you from the land of Egypt, the place of your slavery. "You must not have any other god but me.
>
> "You must not make for yourself an idol of any kind or an image of anything in the heavens or on the earth or in the sea. You must not bow down to them or worship them, for I, the Lord your God, am a jealous God who will not tolerate your affection for any other gods. I lay the sins of the parents upon their children; the entire family is affected—even children in the third and fourth generations of those who reject me. But I lavish unfailing love for a thousand generations on those who love me and obey my commands.
>
> "You must not misuse the name of the Lord your God. The Lord will not let you go unpunished if you misuse his name.
>
> "Remember to observe the Sabbath day by keeping it holy. You have six days each week for your ordinary

work, but the seventh day is a Sabbath day of rest dedicated to the Lord your God. On that day no one in your household may do any work. This includes you, your sons and daughters, your male and female servants, your livestock, and any foreigners living among you. For in six days the Lord made the heavens, the earth, the sea, and everything in them; but on the seventh day he rested. That is why the Lord blessed the Sabbath day and set it apart as holy.

"Honor your father and mother. Then you will live a long, full life in the land the Lord your God is giving you.

"You must not murder.

"You must not commit adultery.

"You must not steal.

"You must not testify falsely against your neighbor.

"You must not covet your neighbor's house. You must not covet your neighbor's wife, male or female servant, ox or donkey, or anything else that belongs to your neighbor."

Jesus summarized the law in two commandments.

"Teacher, which is the greatest commandment in the Law?"

Jesus replied: "'Love the Lord your God with all your heart and with all your soul and with all your mind.' This is the first and greatest commandment. And the second is like it: 'Love your neighbor as yourself.' All the Law and the Prophets hang on these two commandments." Matthew 22:36-40

In the seventh chapter of Matthew, Jesus focused on the commandment commonly called "The Golden Rule."

Golden Rule: *"Do to others whatever you would like them to do to you. This is the essence of all that is taught in the law and the prophets."* Matthew 7:12 (NLT)

The crowd listening to Jesus must have breathed a sigh of relief. Instead of worrying about 613 commandments, Jesus was offering them what golfers would call a "swing reminder." If you just do this, you will succeed. The mood of the crowd probably changed when Jesus immediately transitioned to his discourse on "The Narrow Gate."

The Narrow Gate: *"You can enter God's Kingdom only through the narrow gate. The highway to hell is broad, and its gate is wide for the many who choose that way. But the gateway to life is very narrow and the road is difficult, and only a few ever find it."* Matthew 7:13-14

Many in the crowd must have wondered, "Who are the few? If the gateway to life depended on knowing and following the rules, whether it was 613 Mitovat or just living the Golden Rule, who could ever find salvation?"

The answer was, "No one could maneuver the very narrow and difficult road on their own. The "few" Jesus spoke of were those who chose the route through the narrow gate."

Jesus said, *"I am the gate; whoever enters through me will be saved."* John 10:9a (NIV)

A friend was watching as I hit wayward golf shots, one after another. "What are you focusing on?" He asked.

"I always try to keep my eye on the ball," I responded.

"Pick a dimple on the back of the ball; you need a sharper focal point," he advised.

We also need to sharpen our focus when it comes to our spiritual life. Rather than keeping score based on the good things we have done or the bad things we have avoided doing, we need to focus on finding the narrow gate: Jesus.

Knowing the number of dimples on a golf ball won't make me a better golfer any more than knowing the commandments will make me a better Christian unless they serve to establish my "Moral Par."

The ultimate prize for a golfer is a "hole in one;" the prize for a seeker is to find the Holy One.

"Ask, and it will be given to you; seek, and you will find; knock, and it will be opened to you. For everyone who asks receives, and he who seeks finds, and to him who knocks it will be opened."

MATTHEW 7:7-8 (NASB)

DISARMING YOUR TRIGGERS

I am a terrible speller. If it weren't for spell check on my computer, I'd never get through a paragraph without several misspelled words. Do you know what I need even more than spell-check? I need a "Sin Check"—something that would automatically alert me when I'm about to do something that is wrong. My conscience could be considered a mini-Sin-Check, but conscience has a funny way of going silent when what I'm doing brings me some degree of relief.

Writing in Romans, Saint Paul explained it this way: *For I do not do the good I want to do, but the evil I do not want to do–this I keep on doing.* Romans 7:19 (NIV)

Don't we all face this dilemma? We want to do good, but something deep inside us causes us to sin. Continuing with Romans 7:20, we read, *Now if I do what I do not want to do, it is no longer I who do it, but it is sin living in me that does it.* That's right; our sinful nature takes over.

In John 8:11, Jesus told the woman caught in adultery, *"Go now and leave your life of sin."* I wonder if she, like I, thought, "Easier said than done. Who can help us 'Go and sin no more?'"

It turns out the Holy Spirit acts as the "Sin-Check" I was speaking of earlier.

"But the Advocate, the Holy Spirit, whom the Father will send in my name, will teach you all things and will remind you of everything I have said to you." John 14:26

In our lives, the Holy Spirit warns us when certain sights, sounds, or feelings may trigger sinful responses. Almost any habit, be it good or bad, is initiated by a specific sequence of sensory events. Normally, the sequence is started by a specific sensation called "the trigger." Triggers are sights, sounds, smells, painful memories or even body movements that trigger us to think, say, or do things we know are physically or spiritually harmful. That sounds complicated, but it's important to understand the role of triggers if we want to stop unwanted behaviors.

For example, I used to get extremely angry. One day my son John innocently asked, "Dad, do you know that just before you get angry, your tongue presses against the back of your upper teeth?"

From then on I paid attention, and sure enough, anytime my tongue started to press against my front teeth, I knew anger had started to build in me. Becoming aware of and disarming the trigger allowed me to better control my anger. I still get angry, but if I disengage the trigger (pull my tongue back), I am better able to control my anger.

For me, the trigger was a physical action. For others, it might be a look, a tone of voice, or simply a feeling.

Controlling our triggers is not a matter of will power or "won't" power. We can't do it on our own. Identifying and disarming our personal triggers will only occur when we yield to the healing power of the Holy Spirit in our lives.

The Spirit searches all things, even the deep things of God. For who knows a person's thoughts except their own spirit within them? In the same way no one knows the thoughts of God except the Spirit of God.

1 CORINTHIANS 2:10-11

SOME EXCLUSIONS APPLY

"Love the Lord your God with all your heart and with all your soul and with all your mind and with all your strength. The second is this: 'Love your neighbor as yourself.' There is no commandment greater than these." Mark 12:30-31 (NIV)

Have you ever noticed the fine print on most advertising? Recently I saw a sign in Macy's department store which read: ENTIRE STORE ON SALE! At the bottom of the sign, in words almost too small to be read, was the disclaimer, "Limited Exclusions Apply."

That sign led me to question, "How often do ordinary Christians, like me, have fine print on our commitment to love God." How often, for example, do we apply exclusions when it comes to loving our neighbor as ourselves?

A simple example: one day I was driving to an appointment when I spotted an elderly gentleman standing by the side of the road. A knapsack was slung over his shoulder, and his arm was extended, thumb up, hitchhiking. My first instinct was to pull over and offer him a ride, but I was in the inside turn lane and would have had to maneuver carefully to get to the shoulder. In the amount of time it took for me to check my mirrors, competing thoughts filled my head.

"What if he's dangerous? What if he has farther to go than I need to go? "What if he wants to talk about his problems? Am I prepared to take the time to listen to him?

I stayed in my lane and continued down the road, but a stronger voice seemed to say, *"I tell you the truth when you did it to one of the least of these my brothers and sisters, you were doing it to me!"*

As I made a U-turn, I reluctantly told God I was willing to help, but I sure would appreciate it if someone else would stop to help the man before I reached him. As it turned out, someone who had a more generous concern than me (at that time) had already stopped to offer him a ride.

Now, I'm not encouraging anyone to pick up hitchhikers. In this instance, I felt what I believe was a tug from the Holy Spirit, challenging me to demonstrate, at that moment, how much I love God. Each of us will encounter situations in which the love we show to another is a measure of our love for God.

One of the definitions of love (agapaō) is "to feel or manifest generous concern for another." Do we feel that kind of concern for our neighbors, or do we apply our own "limited exclusions?

In the book, *Love Does*, Bob Goff. mentions that every time he types the word 'love' in a text message, spell-check changes "love" to "live." He concludes, "I learned that fully loving and fully living are not only synonymous, but the kind of life Jesus invited us to be a part of."

Next time you have the chance to send a text message, try typing: "I love you." If your smartphone thinks like mine (or if you tend to fat-finger the keys as I do), it will change "love" to "live"— an electronic reminder that we show our love for God by how we live for Him.

> *No one has ever seen God. But if we love each other, God lives in us, and his love is brought to full expression in us. And God has given us his Spirit as proof that we live in him and he in us.*
>
> 1 JOHN 4:12 (NLT)

CLEAN HOUSE GLASSES

If you could invent something that would make life easier, what would you invent? I'd invent "Clean-House Glasses." Just think of it: a pair of glasses you could have your husband, wife, or friend put on that would totally change their perspective. To the person wearing "Clean-House Glasses," dirty socks on the floor would become invisible, unwashed dishes in the sink would seem to magically disappear, and an automobile that looks like wolves made their dens in the back seat would appear new-car clean.

Of course, once they took off their "Clean-House Glasses," the mess would still be there, and the criticisms would resume. Unless that is, you finally got on the ball and cleaned up your act.

God sees everything. Have you, like me, had times when you *wished* God had "Clean-House Glasses" when it comes to your sin? Times when you knew what you should do but were compelled to take another path? The apostle Paul wrote about this conflict: *I do not understand what I do. For what I want to do I do not do, but what I hate I do. And if I do what I do not want to do, I agree that the law is good. As it is, it is no longer I myself who do it, but it is sin living in me.* Romans 7:15-17 (NIV)

Those of you old enough to remember the comedian Flip Wilson may still smile when you think of his character Geraldine. When Geraldine was caught in an indiscretion, her immediate response would be a high-pitched, "The devil made me do it!"

Neither "It is sin living in me," nor "the devil made me do it" relieve us from the responsibility of our own actions. God doesn't have "Clean-House Glasses" when it comes to sin. He sees and forgives sin, but he wants the messes cleaned up.

God will reward or punish every person for what he has done. Some people live for God's glory, for honor, and for life that has no end. They live for those things by always continuing to do good. God will give life forever to them. But other people are selfish and refuse to follow truth. They follow evil. God will give them his punishment and anger. Romans 2:6-8 (ICB)

The words from Romans would strike terror in our hearts if it weren't for other Scriptures that show that God doesn't have unrealistic expectations.

For everyone has sinned; we all fall short of God's glorious standard. Yet God, in his grace, freely makes us right in his sight. He did this through Christ Jesus when he freed us from the penalty for our sins. Romans 3:23-24 (NLT)

When we fall short of God's standard, it is comforting to know that we have an advocate, Jesus. He is a defender who pleads our case before God.

My dear children, I am writing this to you so that you will not sin. But if anyone does sin, we have an advocate who pleads our case before the Father. He is Jesus Christ, the one who is truly righteous. He himself is the sacrifice that atones for our sins—and not only our sins but the sins of all the world. 1 John 2:1-2

Although we sin, God doesn't give up on us.

And I am certain that God, who began the good work within you, will continue his work until it is finally finished on the day when Christ Jesus returns. Philippians 1:6

Until someone comes along to market "Clean-House Glasses," we'll just have to pick up our socks, wash our dishes, and take a few more trips to the car wash. That will help keep peace in our homes. But trusting in Jesus is the only sure way to keep peace in our hearts.

TAMING THE TONGUE

May the words of my mouth and the meditation of my heart be pleasing to you, O Lord, my rock and my redeemer. Psalm 19:14 (NLT)

Wouldn't it be wonderful if we could filter our words through Psalm 19:14 before we spoke them? Think of the trouble we could avoid.

Indeed, we all make many mistakes, James wrote, *For if we could control our tongues, we would be perfect and could also control ourselves in every other way.* James 3:2

But James made it clear that controlling the tongue is easier said than done: *People can tame all kinds of animals, birds, reptiles, and fish, but no one can tame the tongue. It is restless and evil, full of deadly poison. Sometimes it praises our Lord and Father, and sometimes it curses those who have been made in the image of God.* James 3:7-9

We are uncomfortable with sweeping generalities, so it stops us in our tracks when we read, "No one can tame the tongue." No one? Surely there is someone! With this thought in mind, we are launching a search for that unique individual who has learned to tame the tongue.

How can we recognize that "special" someone who has tamed their tongue? To start, we can narrow our list of candidates by looking for things that suggest a tongue out of control. Turning again to the book of James, we see that boasting, lying, jealousy, and selfishness are all on the "No-No list."

But if you are bitterly jealous and there is selfish ambition in your heart, don't cover up the truth with boasting and lying. James 3:14

Judging others is also contraindicative of a tamed tongue: *Don't speak evil against each other, dear brothers and sisters. If you criticize and judge each other, then you are criticizing and judging God's law. But your job is to obey the law, not to judge whether it applies to you.* James 4:11

Something we all appreciate is self-confidence, but James warns us against boastfulness. *Look here, you who say, "Today or tomorrow we are going to a certain town and will stay there a year. We will do business there and make a profit." What you ought to say is, "If the Lord wants us to, we will live and do this or that."* James 4:13,15

Since we are looking for the person who has learned to control their tongue, we mustn't overlook grumbling. *Don't grumble about each other, brothers and sisters, or you will be judged.* James 5:9a

In 2nd Corinthians 12:20b, the apostle Paul also offered a list of things that would suggest untamed tongues: *quarreling, jealousy, anger, selfishness, slander, gossip, arrogance, and disorderly .behavior.*

We also learn from Paul that what is today accepted as "just boys talking" actually grieves the Holy Spirit. *Do not let any unwholesome talk come out of your mouths, but only what is helpful for building others up according to their needs, that it may benefit those who listen. And do not grieve the Holy Spirit of God, with whom you were sealed for the day of redemption.* Ephesians 4:29-30 (NIV)

Much of what passes as humor today would not pass the "tamed-tongue" test. *Obscene stories, foolish talk, and coarse jokes–these are not for you. Instead, let there be thankfulness to God.* Ephesians 5:4 (NLT)

The apostle James' final addition to our list concerns oaths: *But most of all, my brothers and sisters, never take an oath, by heaven or earth or anything else. Just say a simple yes or no, so that you .will not sin and be condemned. James 5:12*

The poet Carl Sandberg offered this warning: "Be careful with your words, once they are said, they can only be forgiven, not forgotten."

Finally, consider the words from Jude: *But you, dear friends, must build each other up in your most holy faith, pray in the power of the Holy Spirit, and await the mercy of our Lord Jesus Christ, who will bring you eternal life. In this way, you will keep yourselves safe in God's love. Jude 1:20*

ANGER IS A CHOICE

Get rid of all bitterness, rage and anger, brawling and slander, along with every form of malice. Be kind and compassionate to one another, forgiving each other, just as in Christ God forgave you. Ephesians 4:31-32 (NIV)

During a Men's Bible study, the group leader used the above Scripture from Ephesians to kick off a discussion of anger. He was immediately interrupted by one of the men in the group. "You are uniquely unqualified to discuss the topic of anger," the man began. "You aren't married. You don't have children. You're self-employed. You don't drive in rush hour traffic. You don't golf and you don't watch cable news channels. What could you possibly have to get angry about?"

In truth, each of us has a unique set of perceptions that can trigger our anger. At the core of our anger is what the apostle Paul describes in Galatians 5:19 (ICB) as *"sin's control in our lives."*

Of course, there is something known as "righteous indignation," which is justifiable displeasure with anything that is contrary to the will of God. In these instances, it is wise to ask ourselves, "Is it God's will or my self-righteousness indignation that has me all worked up?"

Anger is a choice until we let it become a reflex—when just seeing, hearing, or feeling something can trigger a reaction. Listening to messages by Rick Warren, I learned there are steps we can take that help us short-circuit the anger reflex.

Watch Your Ego

Since we live by the Spirit, let us keep in step with the Spirit. Let us not become conceited, provoking and envying each other. Galatians 5:25-26 (NIV)

Do not think of yourself more highly than you ought, but rather think of yourself with sober judgment, in accordance with the faith God has distributed to each of you. Romans 12:3b

Avoid Foolish Conversations

Do not be quickly provoked in your spirit, for anger resides in the lap of fools. Ecclesiastes 7:9

Slow Down

My dear brothers and sisters, take note of this: Everyone should be quick to listen, slow to speak and slow to become angry, because human anger does not produce the righteousness that God desires. James 1:19-20

Lower the Volume

A gentle answer turns away wrath, but a harsh word stirs up anger. Proverbs 15:1

Watch Your Language

But now you must also rid yourselves of all such things as these: anger, rage, malice, slander, and filthy language from your lips. Colossians 3:8

Choose Friends Carefully

Do not be misled: "Bad company corrupts good character." 1 Corinthians 15:33

. . . Do not make friends with a hot-tempered person, do not associate with one easily angered, or you may learn their ways and get yourself ensnared. Proverbs 22:24-25

Trust God to Right Wrongs

'The LORD is slow to anger, abounding in love and forgiving sin and rebellion. Yet he does not leave the guilty unpunished; Numbers 14:18a

Be Guided by Love

It [love] *does not dishonor others, it is not self-seeking, it is not easily angered, it keeps no record of wrongs.* 1 Corinthians 13:5

Be a Peacemaker

Make every effort to live in peace with everyone and to be holy; without holiness no one will see the Lord. Hebrews 12:14

Make Peace Quickly

"In your anger do not sin": Do not let the sun go down while you are still angry, and do not give the devil a foothold. Ephesians 4:26-27

If All Else Fails, Walk Away

Refrain from anger and turn from wrath; do not fret—it leads only to evil. Psalm 37:8

Anger is a choice. Choose wisely!

JUDGING OTHERS

Anyone who *never* judges others please raise your hand. Seeing no hands raised, especially my own, let's see what the Scriptures tell us about the ubiquitous sin of judging others.

Jesus said, *"Do not judge, or you too will be judged. For in the same way you judge others, you will be judged, and with the measure you use, it will be measured to you."* Matthew 7:1-2 (NIV)

In Colossians 3:13, we are again challenged to avoid judging others: *Bear with each other and forgive one another if any of you has a grievance against someone. Forgive as the Lord forgave you.*

Should we remain silent when we see another taking the wrong path? Are we being judgmental when we offer advice? When we criticize? What standard should we use to draw a line between judging, criticizing and instructing? The Scriptures suggest it depends on your starting point.

The Message Bible offers some clarity: *It's quite simple: Do what is fair and just to your neighbor, be compassionate and loyal in your love, and don't take yourself too seriously—take God seriously."* Micah 6:8b (MSG)

Take God seriously—not yourself—is the starting point. The standard should be what is right or wrong in God's eyes, not what is right or wrong in our "I's. "I think. I want. I need. When we start with God as our perfect guide, we can seek to judge by his standard.

But what if it's an offense that you can't overlook? Jesus tells us, *"If your brother or sister sins, go and point out their fault, just between the two of you. If they listen to you, you have won them over. But if they will not listen, take one or two others along, so that 'every matter may be established by the testimony of two or three witnesses.' If they still refuse to listen, tell it to the church; and if they refuse to listen even to the church, treat them as you would a pagan or a tax collector."* Matthew 18:15-17 *(NIV)*

Of course, there is a right and a wrong way to point out a fault. The Book of Job offers several examples of how not to confront someone. Job's friend Eliphaz's caustic diatribe recorded in the fifteenth chapter is a virtual "how-not-to" on offering someone correction. You know from the opening sentences that Eliphaz missed the part about being compassionate: *"A wise man wouldn't answer with such empty talk! You are nothing but a windbag."* Job 15:2 (NLT)

It went downhill from there.

In his response to Eliphaz, Job gives us a clue as to what righteous criticism might have sounded like: *"I could say the same things if you were in my place. I could spout off criticism and shake my head at you. But if it were me, I would encourage you."* Job 16:4-5a (NLT)

There are times we may feel that political correctness has superseded biblical correctness. Even when we must be critical, our goal should be to encourage the other, as we seek unity and peace.

> *As a prisoner for the Lord, then, I urge you to live a life worthy of the calling you have received. Be completely humble and gentle; be patient, bearing with one another in love. Make every effort to keep the unity of the Spirit through the bond of peace.*
>
> EPHESIANS 4:1-3 (NIV)

LIVE AT PEACE

"Why do you look at the speck of sawdust in your brother's eye and pay no attention to the plank in your own eye? How can you say to your brother, 'Let me take the speck out of your eye,' when all the time there is a plank in your own eye?" Matthew 7:3-4 (NIV)

> *It's in the Book; I know it's true;*
> *to live in peace depends on you.*
> *It took a while for me to see*
> *the "you" involved is really me.*
> *How often have I heard God's word*
> *and misconstrued the things I've heard,*
> *ignored the plank that's in my eye*
> *and found faults in the other guy?*
> *We're all God's kids, I'm sure you've heard.*
> *I know it's true - it's in God's Word.*
> *So, why then do we choose to act,*
> *ignoring that important fact?*
> *If someone wrongs you, don't keep score.*

You've slipped up too, of that I'm sure.
And God forgave you; now confess!
It's wrong to offer others less.
Lord, help us learn to offer grace.
In us, let others see your face.
Inspired by your precious Son,
we'll live at peace with everyone.

If it is possible, as far as it depends on you, live at peace with
everyone.

ROMANS 12:18 (NIV)

ANXIOUS ABOUT EVERYTHING

It started when a couple of numbers in a blood panel came in outside the normal range. Bonnie's physician referred her to hematology. Going against my own best advice, I checked WebMD.com to see what the variance might indicate. Three possible conditions were identified: An infection, OK. An allergy, also OK. The third option, not OK—the "C" word, cancer. Cause for concern.

The weeks until the consultation with the hematologist seemed like forever. Finally, the day came. Bonnie was ushered into an exam room where a wonderful Christian doctor started to explain what the numbers meant and laid out the options. Bonnie could wait several months and retake the blood test, or she could undergo a full-body X-ray and a bone marrow aspiration. The wait-and-test option sounded acceptable until Bonnie glanced at the computer screen and saw the word in bold, red letters: ALERT! More anxiety.

It wasn't until she was on the cold metal table of the X-Ray with the lighted cross mark on her tummy that Bonnie felt the full impact of what was going on. The words of Philippians came to her mind, and she wondered if it really was possible to not be anxious.

Do not be anxious about anything, but in every situation, by prayer and petition, with thanksgiving, present your requests to God. Philippians 4:6 (NIV)

When we face serious challenges, especially when it comes to our health or the health of our loved ones, it's natural to be anxious; it's part of being human. Even Jesus, in his humanity, was anxious as he prayed in the Garden of Gethsemane, *"And being in anguish, he prayed more earnestly, and his sweat was like drops of blood falling to the ground.* Luke 22:44

Feelings aren't a measure of faith; it's how you deal with them. King David, a man after God's heart, asked God to help him with his anxiety: *Search me, God, and know my heart; test me and know my anxious thoughts.* Psalm 139:23

So do not fear, for I am with you; do not be dismayed, for I am your God. I will strengthen you and help you; I will uphold you with my righteous right hand. Isaiah 41:10

On the day of the bone marrow test, we paused to pray before Bonnie went into the treatment room. Holding her olive-wood cross, she prayed."Regardless of the outcome, know I love you, Lord and will never walk away." During the procedure, the words of an old hymn came to her mind. "I have decided to follow Jesus; No turning back, no turning back"

When anxiety was great within me, your consolation brought me joy. Psalm 94:19

Bonnie jokingly says, "Worry works; most things we worry about never happen."

The hematologist said it would be two or three weeks until we'd have the results, but he didn't think there would be anything to worry about. As it turned out, there was nothing to worry about.

Of course, things don't always turn out the way we want them to. Sometimes the test comes back positive; sometimes the loved one doesn't get better. We may not understand, but *we know that in all things God works for the good of those who love him, who have been called according to his purpose.* Romans 8:28

Are you anxious? *Cast all your anxiety on him because he cares for you.* 1 Peter 5:7

Recently Bonnie was talking to a woman who had been diagnosed with cancer. "I feel bad because I am a Christian and I'm not supposed to be anxious about anything."

Bonnie hugged her and confided, "I'm anxious about everything! God knows we can get caught in the revolving door of anxiety, Thankfully, God is always there waiting for us to receive His peace."

> *So do not fear, for I am with you; do not be dismayed, for I am your God. I will strengthen you and help you; I will uphold you with my righteous right hand.*
>
> ISAIAH 41:10 (NIV)

STRESS TEST

When I started to feel symptoms that suggested I might be on the verge of a heart attack, I asked Bonnie to take me to the emergency room. An EKG and a blood test pretty much ruled out a heart problem, but for safety's sake, I was kept in the hospital overnight so I could take a stress test in the morning. The stress test was also negative. It turned out that lousy pizza and an unusually stressful day had probably caused my body to say, "Enough!"

Sometimes, we can find ourselves so focused on what's going wrong in our lives that we overlook all that has been going right. We may begin to wonder if God even cares. In times like this, our best course of action is to do as the Psalmist did:

In the opening verses, you can feel the tension. The Psalmist fervently prayed to God for help.

I cried out to God for help;
I cried out to God to hear me.
When I was in distress, I sought the Lord;
at night I stretched out untiring hands,
and I would not be comforted.
I remembered you, God, and I groaned;
I meditated, and my spirit grew faint.
You kept my eyes from closing;
I was too troubled to speak.

Psalm 77:1-4 (NIV)

In the verses that follow, when the Psalmist compared his present state to times when things were better, he wondered if God had rejected him. When we compare our "what was" with our "what is," we, too, can begin to wonder where God is.

I thought about the former days,
the years of long ago;
I remembered my songs in the night.
My heart meditated and my spirit asked:
"Will the Lord reject forever?
Will he never show his favor again?
Has his unfailing love vanished forever?
Has his promise failed for all time?
Has God forgotten to be merciful?
Has he in anger withheld his compassion?"

Psalm 77:5-9

Now, notice in the following verses how the Psalmist's stress level dropped when he changed his focus from his present problems to what God had done in the past:

I will remember the deeds of the LORD;
yes, I will remember your miracles of long ago.
I will consider all your works
and meditate on all your mighty deeds."

Your ways, God, are holy.
What god is as great as our God?
You are the God who performs miracles;
you display your power among the peoples.

Psalm 77:11-14

There will be times when we feel our prayers haven't been answered. We may have times when life seems unfair! And yes, we may even have times when we feel God has abandoned us. In those times, it is important to remember who God is, to remember what He has done, and most important to remember what He still can accomplish.

Bonnie offered, "God has given me more than my prayers could have ever asked for."

Now all glory to God, who is able, through his mighty power
at work within us, to accomplish infinitely more than we
might ask or think.

EPHESIANS 3:20 (NLT)

PRUNING TIME

"I am the true grapevine, and my Father is the gardener. He cuts off every branch of mine that doesn't produce fruit, and he prunes the branches that do bear fruit so they will produce even more. You have already been pruned and purified by the message I have given you. Remain in me, and I will remain in you. For a branch cannot produce fruit if it is severed from the vine, and you cannot be fruitful unless you remain in me." John 15:1-4 (NLT)

On first reading, John 15:1-4 can be a disturbing Scripture. What does Jesus mean when he says, *"He cuts off every branch of mine* that doesn't bear fruit?" Does that mean God has given each of us a "to-do" list that must be completed or "snip, snip"?

Thankfully, that's not the way it works. In the Reformation Study Bible, R.C. Sproul explains, "No branch that is in Christ can be wholly fruitless. But branches that belong to Christ will bear fruit and undergo the pruning necessary to increase. ('Fruit' refers to a Christ-like life produced by the Holy Spirit.)"

But the Holy Spirit produces this kind of fruit in our lives: love, joy, peace, patience, kindness, goodness, faithfulness, gentleness, and self-control. There is no law against these things! Galatians 5:22-23

God doesn't have a "to do" list; He has more of a "to be" list. Yes, we all need pruning, but guided by the Holy Spirit, we can learn to be more like Jesus. Then, we'll have a new "to do" list.

"To Do" List for Today

✓ Love God
✓ Love People

"A Prayer to the Gardener"

God is the gardener, Jesus the vine.
Lord, help your branches to grow.
Blessed and caressed by your Spirit divine,
we'll share your love where we go.
Prune us and shape us to be more like you;
make us more fruitful each day.
Fed by your word, we'll continue to grow,
as we show others the way.
No one can save us, save Jesus our Lord.
He is the truth and the way.
Joined to the true vine, his branches will grow;
Lord, draw us closer today.
AMEN

DO THIS IN REMEMBRANCE

> *On the night when he was betrayed, the Lord Jesus
> took some bread and gave thanks to God for it. Then
> he broke it in pieces and said, "This is my body,
> which is given for you. Do this in remembrance of
> me." In the same way, he took the cup of wine after
> supper, saying, "This cup is the new covenant be-
> tween God and his people–an agreement confirmed
> with my blood. Do this in remembrance of me as
> often as you drink it." For every time you eat this
> bread and drink this cup, you are announcing the
> Lord's death until he comes again.* 1 Corinthians
> 11:23b-26 (NLT)

The congregation at the Saddleback chapel service at Park Terrace has attendees from several religious traditions. Evangelicals
join with Catholics, Presbyterians, Baptists, Episcopalians, and
others to praise God, share the Good News of Jesus Christ, and
love one another.

About once a month, we celebrate what some call the "Eucharist," what others refer to as the "Lord's Supper," and what still
others call "Communion."

For those who aren't familiar with the terms: Eucharist comes
from the Greek word *eucharistia*, meaning thanksgiving. The Lord
Jesus took some bread and gave thanks (*eucharisteō*) to God for it.

Communion (or sharing) is a translation of the Greek word
koinonia. When we bless the cup at the Lord's Table, we are sharing
(*koinonia*) in the blood of Christ. And when we break the bread, we
are sharing in the body of Christ.

During communion, we come together to share a meal, with
thanksgiving, at which we remember the sacrifice Jesus made for
each of us. Communion is not just about remembering; it is also a
time to recommit to the covenant we have made with God to be His
people. "*This cup is the new covenant between God and his people–an*

agreement confirmed with my blood, which is poured out as a sacrifice for you." Luke 22:20b

The word Sacrament may not familiar to you. Traditionally, a Sacrament is an act Jesus commanded his followers to do and which he himself did. Baptism, fasting, and communion would be recognized as Sacraments.

Because communion is associated with Jesus' death, it commands a high level of respect. When we are given the elements, we are to take them reverently, with gratitude for Christ's sacrifice.

One part of Scripture that is not emphasized as much as it should be is 1st Corinthians 11:27 which reads, *So then, whoever eats the bread or drinks the cup of the Lord in an unworthy manner will be guilty of sinning against the body and blood of the Lord.*

Communion can serve as a checkpoint to see how well we are doing in our walk with the Lord. It's a perfect time to check the three "P's"— Prayer, Praise, and Proclamation. Are we turning to God in prayer? Are we praising Him for all he has done for us? Are we proclaiming Jesus as Lord in our lives?

Holocaust survivor Corrie Ten Boom reportedly prayed about everything. One time she needed a new pair of shoes, so she prayed before she went shopping. When she came home, she pulled out the shoes and said, "Look what God has given me." That small expression of gratitude was just one example of Corrie Ten Boom's commitment to walk with God daily. Does our daily life evidence our commitment to the Lord? What do we do in remembrance of Him?

Commit your way to the LORD; trust in him and he will do this: He will make your righteous reward shine like the dawn, your vindication like the noonday sun.

PSALM 37:5-6 (NIV)

A SPIRITUAL FITNESS PLAN

NO ONE HAS EVER SEEN GOD. BUT IF WE LOVE EACH OTHER,
GOD LIVES IN US, AND HIS LOVE IS BROUGHT
TO FULL EXPRESSION IN US.
AND GOD HAS GIVEN US HIS SPIRIT AS PROOF
THAT WE LIVE IN HIM AND HE IN US.

1 John 4:12 (NLT)

USING YOUR SPIRITUAL FITBIT

Millions of Americans have joined the Fitbit® craze. Just in case you're not into the latest tech-gadgets, let me explain what a Fitbit is. A Fitbit is a pendant or wristwatch-size device that monitors your physical activity and motivates you to do more.

Fitbit fans establish goals for the number of hours they sleep, the number of steps they take, and the number of calories they burn. It is not unusual to see a Fitbit fan jogging in front of the television set or refusing to go to bed until they reach their 10,000-step goal. One "Fitbit aficionado" we know, kidding, asked a friend to wear *her* Fitbit, explaining that she was running behind her step goal and needed help catching up.

One of the essential elements in any fitness program is keeping track of your progress. In fact, the apostle Paul probably would have owned a 1st Century "Fitus-Bitus" if such a device had been available. Paul wrote, *I discipline my body like an athlete, training it to do what it should.* 1 Corinthians 9:27a (NLT) "

Of course, the apostle placed a much higher priority on measuring spiritual fitness. All *athletes are disciplined in their training. They do it to win a prize that will fade away, but we do it for an eternal prize. So I run with purpose in every step.* 1 Corinthians 9:25-26a

How can we keep track of our spiritual fitness? Is there a metaphorical "Spiritual Fitbit" we can rely on to help us measure the steps we take towards God each day? There is; it's our Bible.

I can't count how many times I would visit my grandmother Alice and find her sitting in her lounge chair carefully reading her Bible. The pages were dog-eared, and so many passages were highlighted that you figured you might as well read the whole page. She took Psalm 119:105 seriously. *Your word is a lamp to guide my feet and a light for my path.* Grandma Alice's Bible showed that her favorite exercise was spiritual jogging.

By contrast, we can be like the "Fitbit aficionado" referenced above who suggested someone else might be able to take her steps for her. Our Spiritual Fitbit, our Bible, needs to be part of our daily routine. If our only exposure to the Word is on Sunday, our Spiritual Fitbit needs recharging.

> For we have the living Word of God, which is full of energy, and it pierces more sharply than a two-edged sword. . . . It interprets and reveals the true thoughts and secret motives of our hearts.

HEBREWS 4:12 (TPT)

SPIRITUAL FITNESS PLAN: PRAYER

In the previous section, we looked at ways we can make reading the Bible the cornerstone of our Spiritual Fitness Plan. If we want to step closer to God, it simply makes sense to spend more time reading the Book that will help us keep from stumbling.

The next exercise in our Spiritual Fitness Plan is prayer. In Ephesians 6:18 (NLT), the apostle Paul directed the Ephesians, *Pray in the Spirit at all times and on every occasion. Stay alert and be persistent in your prayers for all believers everywhere.*

In 1st Thessalonians 5:16-18, he proclaimed, *Always be joyful. Never stop praying. Be thankful in all circumstances, for this is God's will for you who belong to Christ Jesus.*

Taking time to pray isn't something we should do occasionally; it is something we need to do while we are doing everything else. Making daily prayer part of our Spiritual Fitness Plan can help us deal with our past, find guidance for our present, and build hope for the future.

God once said, "Let the light shine out of the darkness!" And this is the same God who made his light shine in our hearts. He gave us light by letting us know the glory of God that is in the face of Christ. 2 Corinthians 4:6 (ICB)

Rather than focusing on the path in front of us, we can become so preoccupied with the "would have," "could have," and "should have" that we become blind to how far we have come. And we have come a long way: *Anyone who belongs to Christ has become a new person. The old life is gone; a new life has begun!* 2 Corinthians 5:17b (NLT)

Do you need assurance that God loves you despite the things you may have done . . . or things that may have been done to you? Take your concerns to God in prayer and trust His answers.

In her book *Uninvited: Living Life When You Feel Less Than, Left Out, and Lonely,* Lysa TerKeurst writes, "God's love isn't based on me; it's placed on me." Later she explains, "He waits every day with every answer we need, every comfort we crave, every affection we're desperate for, while we look everywhere else but at Him.

"*We run at a breakneck pace to try and achieve what God simply wants us to slow down enough to receive. Fully. Completely. Perfectly. In Him. With Him. By Him.* We just need to turn to Him. And sit with Him. No matter what."

In John 15:7 (ICB), Jesus spoke about the perfect Spiritual Fitness Plan: "*Remain in me and follow my teachings. If you do this, then you can ask for anything you want, and it will be given to you.*".

SPIRITUAL FITNESS PLAN: FORGIVENESS

Every spiritual fitness plan also needs to look at forgiveness. Jesus spoke of this stumbling block when he taught his disciples to pray, "*Forgive us our sins, as we have forgiven those who sin against us.*" Matthew 6:12 (NLT)

Jesus goes on to say, "*If you forgive those who sin against you, your heavenly Father will forgive you. But if you refuse to forgive others, your Father will not forgive your sins.*" Matthew 6:14-15

Jesus repeated this warning, "*I tell you, you can pray for anything, and if you believe that you've received it, it will be yours. But when you are praying, first forgive anyone you are holding a grudge against, so that your Father in heaven will forgive your sins, too."* Mark 11:24-25

We can have "mountain-moving" power, but that kind of power is activated by faith and contingent on forgiveness. Our path to forgiveness begins with our confession of our own sins, but the stumbling block for many is forgiveness of the sins of others.

This section has been the most difficult for me to write. Forgiving others doesn't come easy. When someone has hurt one of my loved ones, my first impulse is to want to strike back. Then, I read: *Dear friends, never take revenge. Leave that to the righteous anger of God. For the Scriptures say, "I will take revenge; I will pay them back," says the Lord.* R.omans 12:19

Aren't there some offenses so egregious as to be unforgivable? Do we really have to forgive everyone? How far are we expected to go with our forgiveness? If I can't strike back, can I at least walk away? I raise these questions because I'm pretty sure I'm not the only one who has struggled to understand what Jesus meant when he said, *". . . as we forgive others."*

When we want to better understand the verses of Scripture, it can be helpful to read different translations to see how different translation teams have interpreted the original text. Approach using different translations in the spirit of Psalm 86:11: *Teach me your ways, O LORD, that I may live according to your truth! Grant me purity of heart, so that I may honor you.*

This is very different from the approach of comedian W.C. Fields who, on his deathbed, was found reading the Bible. When a friend asked him what was going in, he replied, "Looking for loopholes." I've gone through quite a few different translations and must report there are no loopholes when it comes to forgiving others.

There are times when we might not think it is fair to forgive, times when we want God to punish, but forgiveness isn't about fairness; it's about God's grace.

Be kind and loving to each other. Forgive each other just as God forgave you in Christ. Ephesians 4:32 (ICB)

How far we go when it comes to forgiving others may be a measure of how far we have come in our effort to come closer to God. I may not have it in my heart to forgive someone who has committed a heinous crime. With God's help, I may find the grace to at least pray for them. I may have been hurt so badly that I cannot fellowship with someone, but I must still pray for them.

This is the prayer Bonnie and I turn to when we struggle with forgiveness: Lord, I do not feel compassion for the person I have been asked to pray for, but I know you do. Please help them, and help me to change.

Let the wicked forsake their ways and the unrighteous their thoughts. Let them turn to the Lord, and he will have mercy on them, and to our God, for he will freely pardon. Isaiah 55:7 (NIV)

In our daily lives, forgiving others is another way of living the golden rule: "*Do unto others as you would like them to do to you. If you love only those who love you, why should you get credit for that? Even sinners love those who love them! And if you do good only to those who do good to you, why should you get credit? Even sinners do that much!*" Luke 6:31-33 (NLT)

Translations that use the words, debts, trespasses, offenses, etc. (in lieu of sin) show that even small offenses give us daily opportunities to forgive.

Love prospers when a fault is forgiven, but dwelling on it separates close friends. Proverbs 17:9

When we forgive our family, our neighbors, and our brothers and sisters in Christ, we find peace for our souls and bring glory to God.

Finally, brothers and sisters, rejoice! Strive for full restoration, encourage one another, be of one mind, live in peace. And the God of love and peace will be with you.

2 CORINTHIANS 13:11 (NIV)

SPIRITUAL FITNESS PLAN: FASTING

Following Church traditions, many Christians use a period of prayer and fasting to come to a deeper appreciation of the sacrifices Jesus made to pave the way for our salvation. Fasting is biblical, being mentioned in the following verses:

Exodus 34:28	Psalm 69:10
Numbers 29:7	Psalm 109:24
Judges 20:26	Isaiah 58:3-6
1 Samuel 7:6 ; 31:13	Jeremiah 14:12
2 Samuel 1:12; 12:16, 22-32	Jeremiah 36:6-9
1 Kings 21:9,12	Daniel 9:3
1 Chronicles 10:2; 20:3	Joel 1:14
2 Chronicles 20:3	Joel 2:12-15
Ezra 8:21,23	Jonah 3:5
Nehemiah 1:4; 9:1	Zechariah 7:1-5
Esther 4:3, 16; 9:31	Zechariah 8:19
Psalm 35:13	Luke 2:37
Matthew 4:2	Luke 5:33-35
Matthew 6:16-18	Luke 18:12
Matthew 9:14-15	Acts 13:2-3
Mark 2:18-20	Acts 14:23

The only time fasting is commanded is in Numbers 29:7, where fasting is one of the offerings listed for the Day of Atonement.

In the Scriptures, fasting is closely tied with prayer and repentance. When we voluntarily give up something for Lent, for instance, the goal is to switch our focus from earthly pleasures to the joy we will inherit because of Jesus' sacrifice on the cross.

As far back as I can remember, my mother made a habit of giving up ice cream for Lent. As a young boy that seemed extreme to me. Giving up Brussel sprouts was more like it. Over the years, I've heard of people giving up certain foods, their favorite television or radio program, or even taking a hiatus from playing a favorite game or sport. One friend shared how she gave up Starbucks and used the money she saved as a special offering for the homeless.

Others, as an act of repentance and renewal, choose to give up bad habits. They concentrate on not doing the "Do Nots."

- **Do not** *follow the crowd in doing wrong.* Exodus 23:2a
- *In your anger do not sin:* **Do not** *let the sun go down while you are still angry,* Ephesians 4:26
- **Do not** *lie to each other, since you have taken off your old self with its practices* Colossians 3:9
- *Husbands, love your wives and* **do not** *be harsh with them.* Colossians 3:19

Unfortunately, a lot of what passes for fasting can be more of a physical or mental fitness exercise. If our goal in fasting is to lose weight or save money, we may have missed the point. In fasting, the focus should be on God, not on ourselves. In Isaiah, we learn that the Israelites earned God's displeasure by doing the "right thing" for the "wrong reasons."

'Why have we fasted,' they say, 'and you have not seen it? Why have we humbled ourselves, and you have not noticed?' [The Israelites expected a quid pro quo.]

Yet on the day of your fasting, you do as you please and exploit all your workers. Your fasting ends in quarreling and strife, and in striking each other with wicked fists. You cannot fast as you do today and expect your voice to be heard on high. Is this the kind of fast I have chosen, only a day for people to humble themselves? Is it only for bowing one's head like a reed and for lying in sackcloth and ashes? Is that what you call a fast, a day acceptable to the Lord? Isaiah 58:3-4, 5b

Continuing in Isaiah, we see that God responds to hearts that are loving and compassionate.

"Is not this the kind of fasting I have chosen: to loose the chains of injustice and untie the cords of the yoke, to set the oppressed free and break every yoke?

Is it not to share your food with the hungry and to provide the poor wanderer with shelter—when you see the naked, to clothe them, and not to turn away from your own flesh and blood?

Then your light will break forth like the dawn, and your healing will quickly appear; then your righteousness will go before you, and the glory of the Lord will be your rear guard. Then you will call, and the Lord will answer; you will cry for help, and he will say: Here am I." Isaiah 58:6

When we fast, we humble ourselves to show God we love Him. It's not what we say that matters, it's what we do. *Dear children, let us not love with words or speech but with actions and in truth.* 1 John 3:18

The next time I fast, I won't be giving up Brussel sprouts. Instead, I will be praying God will show me what he desires from me. After all, it's not what we *give up* that matters; what matters is that we are willing to humble ourselves and *give over* control of our lives to God.

BUILDING A SPIRITUAL FITNESS TEAM

God's love is wonderfully contagious. The more we spread it around, the more we feel it growing in our lives. Of course, before we can share God's love, we need to feel it operating in our lives. In this book, we have tried to address ways to prepare our hearts and minds to feel the presence of God. Throughout, we have used God's Word as a template upon which to build our faith. We have used stories from our experiences to demonstrate the life-changing difference sharing God's love can make in our lives. Whether you are new to Christianity or a life-long believer, it is wise to exercise your spiritual muscles. Don't let your faith atrophy; keep it growing with a Spiritual Fitness Plan.

Know your Coach

The Bible is just another great book until it becomes our "Playbook for Life." That begins to happen when we open our hearts to the coaching of the Holy Spirit.

Jesus said, *"But the Advocate, the Holy Spirit, whom the Father will send in my name, will teach you all things and will remind you of everything I have said to you."* John 14:26 (NIV)

Set your goals

We need to make sure we have set the right spiritual goals. If we wish to grow spiritually, we should rely on the one Book that will show us the right path.

Show me your ways, Lord, teach me your paths. Guide me in your truth and teach me, for you are God my Savior, and my hope is in you all day long. Psalm 25:4-5

Build a team

Plans fail for lack of counsel, but with many advisers they succeed. Proverbs 15:22

Listen to advice and accept discipline, and at the end you will be counted among the wise. Proverbs 19:20

As iron sharpens iron, so one person sharpens another. Proverbs 27:17

The above Scriptures remind us that a support team can help us move toward improved spiritual fitness. Joining a small group or participating in a Bible study can put you in contact with others who are taking important steps towards God.

Set aside time

It is also important to set aside specific times to work on our spiritual health. One couple we know has a period of devotions each morning and prayers of thanksgiving at bedtime.

In Ecclesiastes 3:1 we are reminded, *There is a time for everything, and a season for every activity under the heavens.*

The Psalmist offered: *It is good to give thanks to the Lord, to sing praises to the Most High. It is good to proclaim your unfailing love in the morning, your faithfulness in the evening. Psalm 92:1-2* (NLT)

Add resources

When you're ready to kick your spiritual workout into high gear, there are a plethora of resources you can tap into:

1. Today, most churches have sermon archives and/or small group studies on their websites.
2. There is a wide variety of devotionals such as Oswald Chambers' *My Utmost for His Highest*, Max Lucado's *Grace for the Moment*, Ellie Claire's *Daily in his Presence*, and Sarah Young's *Jesus Calling*, to name a few.
3. Study Bibles, Reading Plans, and Commentaries, such as *Matthew Henry's Commentary* and the *Reformation Study Bible*, can help you gain a deeper understanding of what you read in the Scriptures.
4. If you have access to the internet, www.biblegateway.com offers 54 different English translations of the Bible.
5. Tune to Christian radio stations such as KBRITE—740 AM in Southern California. Use the website www.christianradio.com/stations/ to find a Christian radio station in your area.
6. There are audio versions of the Bible that you can play on your iPhone or Mp3 player as you work out.
7. The Museum of the Bible in Washington, D.C. is a monument to the Glory of God. https://www.museumofthebible.org/

8. Perhaps you would like to share with others some of the steps you are taking that bring you closer to God. We encourage you to leave a comment on our website: www.becausehelovesus-press.com.

> *The Lord directs the steps of the godly. He delights in every detail of their lives.*
>
> PSALM 37:23

RESOLUTIONS

The website YouGov.com surveyed Americans to learn what resolutions people were committing to in 2019. Respondents could include more than one in their responses.
Here's the list:

- Eat better—37 percent
- Exercise more 37— percent
- Spend less money—37 percent
- Self-care (e.g. getting more sleep)—24 percent
- Read more books—18 percent
- Learn a new skill—15 percent
- Get a new job—14 percent
- Make new friends—13 percent
- New hobby—13 percent
- Focus more on appearance—12 percent
- Focus on relationship—12 percent
- Cut down on cigarettes/alcohol—9 percent
- Go on more dates—7 percent
- Focus less on appearance—3 percent

The following are the same resolutions as a Christian might think about them.

- Eat better—*Man does not live on bread alone but on every word that comes from the mouth of the LORD.* Deuteronomy 8:3b (NIV)
- Exercise more—*For physical training is of some value, but godliness has value for all things, holding promise for both the present life and the life to come.* 1 Timothy 4:8
- Spend less money—*I am not saying this because I am in need, for I have learned to be content whatever the circumstances.* Philippians 4:11
- Get more sleep—*In peace I will lie down and sleep, for you alone, LORD, make me dwell in safety.* Psalm 4:8
- Read more books—*For the Word of God is alive and active. Sharper than any double-edged sword, it penetrates even to dividing soul and spirit, joints and marrow; it judges the thoughts and attitudes of the heart.* Hebrews 4:12
- Learn a new skill—*Bless all his skills, LORD, and be pleased with the work of his hands.* Deuteronomy 33:11
- Get a new job—*Whatever you do, work at it with all your heart, as working for the Lord, not for human masters.* Colossians 3:23
- Make new friends—*The righteous choose their friends carefully, but the way of the wicked leads them astray.* Proverbs 12:26
- New hobby—*There is a time for everything, and a season for every activity under the heavens.* Ecclesiastes 3:1
- Focus on appearance—*"The LORD does not look at the things people look at. People look at the outward appearance, but the LORD looks at the heart."* 1 Samuel 16:7b
- Focus on relationship—*In your relationships with one another, have the same mindset as Christ Jesus: Who, being in very nature God, did not consider equality with God something to be used to his own advantage; rather, he made himself nothing by taking the very nature of a servant, being made in human likeness.* Philippians 2:5-7

- Cut down on cigarettes/alcohol—*Do you not know that your bodies are temples of the Holy Spirit, who is in you, whom you have received from God? You are not your own; you were bought at a price. Therefore honor God with your bodies.* 1 Corinthians 6:19-20
- Go on more dates—*Do not be yoked together with unbelievers. For what do righteousness and wickedness have in common? Or what fellowship can light have with darkness?* 2 Corinthians 6:14
- Focus less on appearance—*"And why do you worry about clothes? See how the flowers of the field grow. They do not labor or spin. Yet I tell you that not even Solomon in all his splendor was dressed like one of these.?"* Matthew 6:28-29

My 87-year old sister offered two resolutions that she felt would help her have a better year. Those are resolutions most of us can commit to.

1. Have more patience. *The end of a matter is better than its beginning, and patience is better than pride.* Ecclesiastes 7:8
2. Give Jesus a bigger share of my heart. *But be sure to fear the LORD and serve him faithfully with all your heart; consider what great things he has done for you.* 1 Samuel 12:24

NEST EGG OR GOOSE EGG?

After some general conversation, our new financial advisor posed the question, "What is your primary objective?" Without missing a beat, Bonnie responded, "To make sure our 'nest egg' doesn't become a 'goose egg'!"

Later we started to wonder, "What about our 'spiritual nest egg'?" When we get to heaven, what will we have 'paid forward'?" As part of the Sermon on the Mount, Jesus spoke about storing up treasures in heaven: *"Do not store up for yourselves treasures on earth, where moths and vermin destroy, and where thieves break in and steal. But store up for yourselves treasures in heaven . . . For where your treasure is, there your heart will be also."* Matthew 6:19-21 (NIV)

Since no one gets to take a U-Haul with them to heaven, what is the treasure Jesus was talking about? The treasure is found in our relationship with Christ.

"My goal is that they may be encouraged in heart and united in love, so that they may have the full riches of complete understanding, in order that they may know the mystery of God, namely, Christ, in whom are hidden all the treasures of wisdom and knowledge." Colossians 2:2-3

The treasures are wisdom and knowledge found in Christ Jesus. The more we come to know him, the more we can be encouraged and united in love with other believers.

What impact does this have? Paul writes, *So then, just as you received Christ Jesus as Lord, continue to live your lives in him, rooted and built up in him, strengthened in the faith as you were taught, and overflowing with thankfulness.* Colossians 2:6-7

In God's economy, a treasure is not to be hoarded but shared. Let us join with the apostle Paul in praying for opportunities to share the good news:

Devote yourselves to prayer with an alert mind and a thankful heart. Pray for us, too, that God will give us many opportunities to speak about his mysterious plan concerning Christ.

Live wisely among those who are not believers, and make the most of every opportunity. Let your conversation be gracious and attractive so that you will have the right response for everyone. Colossians 4:2-3a, 5-6 (NLT)

Our financial advisors can help us avoid turning our "nest eggs" into "goose eggs," but the spiritual "nest egg" we leave to our family, friends and to others will grow as our love of Christ increases.

And this same God who takes care of me will supply all your needs from his glorious riches, which have been given to us in Christ Jesus.

PHILIPPIANS 4:19

BETWEEN THE ADVENTS

In his book, *Because of Bethlehem*, Max Lucado reminds us, "We live between the Advents." We know the approximate date of Jesus' birth, but as for the Second Coming, Jesus tells us, *"But about that day or hour no one knows, not even the angels in heaven, nor the Son, but only the Father."* Matthew 24:36 (NIV)

Of course, many of those who engage in eschatology (the study of end times) look at the signs of our times and believe that Jesus' return is just around the corner. Their arguments notwithstanding, for any of us, the end time may be just beyond the next sunrise. Which leads to an interesting question, "What would you do today if you knew for certain that you would meet Jesus tomorrow?"

Now there are flippant answers, and there are theological answers to that question. The flippant answers can be fun, so let's consider some of them first.

"If I knew I'd meet Jesus tomorrow, the politician might say, "That's one recall I'll be glad to be a part of."

"If I knew I'd meet Jesus tomorrow, an overeater might respond, "I'd have a large banana split and a sheet cake, with one fork. I'll deal with the weightier issues tomorrow."

"If I knew I'd meet Jesus tomorrow, the atheist might say, 'Jesus? Jesus who?"

The atheist's response actually moves us from the flippant to theological. Jesus wants to know who we say he is.

Jesus and his disciples went on to the villages around Caesarea Philippi. On the way he asked them, "Who do people say I am?"

They replied, "Some say John the Baptist; others say Elijah; and still others, one of the prophets."

"But what about you?" he asked. "Who do you say I am?"'

Peter answered, "You are the Messiah Mark 8:27-29

We find the answer to Jesus' "Who am I?" question in the words spoken to the shepherds: *And the angel said unto them, "Fear not: for, behold, I bring you good tidings of great joy, which shall be to all people. For unto you is born this day in the city of David a Savior, which is Christ the Lord."* Luke 2:10-11 (KJV)

Who you say Jesus is will determine how you anticipate the Second Advent. With this in mind, if I knew for certain I was going to meet the Lord tomorrow, I don't think I'd be too concerned about today. I pray my focus would be on getting ready for that glorious tomorrow.

Therefore, God elevated him to the place of highest honor and gave him the name above all other names, that at the name of Jesus every knee should bow, in heaven and on earth and under the earth, and every tongue declare that Jesus Christ is Lord, to the glory of God the Father. PHILIPPIANS 2:9-11 (NLT)

"A Better Day is Coming"

From chickenpox to cataracts
from Pampers to Depends,
So goes the cycle we call life;
As it begins, it ends.
No need to moan when arches fall
or wrinkles cross your face.
So what, if you have lost a step?
There is no need to race.
Accept your skin that has more spots
and hair that's snowy white.
Accept the fact that now you must
wake up to pee at night.
Rejoice when you forget the things
You used to know by heart.
Rejoice that heaven's closer,
where you'll get a brand-new start.

White hair is a crown of glory and is seen most among the godly.

PROVERBS 16:31 (TLB)

LOOKING FORWARD TO HEAVEN

Bonnie and I stood at the bedside of Bill, a 95-year-old friend, who was in hospice care. He was tucked comfortably in his covers. His face radiated peace, peace, as we read about in Philippians, that passes all understanding—a peace that, for Bill, came from having had a life-long relationship with the Lord.

We prayed for him, asking God to make his transition as easy as possible. Bill had looked forward to joining his beloved wife Geneva in heaven, but I suspect when it comes to heaven, meeting a loved one will be one great joy in the midst of a never-ending "Hallelujah." Yes, Bill was on the threshold of seeing Geneva. Even better, he would be meeting Jesus.

Much of what the Bible has to say about heaven is metaphorical or symbolic. I'll leave it to Christian eschatologists to decipher the book of Revelation. Thankfully, we know quite a bit about heaven based on other Scriptures. In one of his small group studies, Rick Warren outlined some of the things the Bible tells us about heaven.

There is a ticket to heaven: Jesus. *Jesus told him, "I am the way, the truth, and the life. No one can come to the Father except through me."* John 14:6 (NLT)

Jesus is looking for true disciples. *"Not everyone who calls out to me, 'Lord! Lord!' will enter the Kingdom of Heaven. Only those who actually do the will of my Father in heaven will enter.»* Matthew 7:21

There is a difference between being judged and judgment.

For we must all stand before Christ to be judged. We will each receive whatever we deserve for the good or evil we have done in this earthly body. 2 Corinthians 5:10

"And anyone who believes in God's Son has eternal life. Anyone who doesn't obey the Son will never experience eternal life but remains under God's angry judgment." John 3:36

Rewards in heaven will be based on our motives on Earth. *"But when you demonstrate generosity, do it with pure motives and without drawing attention to yourself. Give secretly and your Father, who sees all you do, will reward you openly."* Matthew 6:3-4 (TPT)

A place has been prepared. *"There is more than enough room in my Father's home. If this were not so, would I have told you that I am going to prepare a place for you?"* John 14:2 (NLT)

Followers of Christ will get an amazing "make-over." *For we know that when this earthly tent we live in is taken down (that is, when we die and leave this earthly body), we will have a house in heaven, an eternal body made for us by God himself and not by human hands.* 2 Corinthians 5:1

A great reward awaits those persecuted for following Jesus. *"God blesses you when people mock you and persecute you and lie about you and say all sorts of evil things against you because you are my followers. Be happy about it! Be very glad! For a great reward awaits you in heaven. And remember, the ancient prophets were persecuted in the same way."* Matthew 5:11-12

Heaven is forever. *Day by day the LORD takes care of the innocent, and they will receive an inheritance that lasts forever.* Psalm 37:18

There is no waiting period for the spirit of those who die in Christ! *And Jesus replied, "I assure you, today you will be with me in paradise."* Luke 23:43

Whenever anyone asks me what I believe heaven will be like, I make the mistake of thinking in human terms. I imagine myself sitting by a beautiful stream watching God paint a rainbow or listening as he assigns one of His angels the task of being air traffic control for a flight of birds. You may think about sitting with loved ones, sharing memories, and enjoying the smells and tastes around the banquet table Jesus has laid out for us, a banquet table with all our favorite goodies. We can only imagine.

Scriptures tell us our thinking is way too small.

"My thoughts are nothing like your thoughts," says the LORD. "And my ways are far beyond anything you could imagine." Isaiah 55:8

That is what the Scriptures mean when they say, "No eye has seen, no ear has heard, and no mind has imagined what God has prepared for those who love him." 1 Corinthians 2:9

And [we] pray that Christ will be more and more at home in your hearts, living within you as you trust in him. May your roots go down deep into the soil of God's marvelous love; and may you be able to feel and understand, as all God's children should, how long, how wide, how deep, and how high his love really is; and to experience this love for yourselves, though it is so great that you will never see the end of it or fully know or understand it. And so at last you will be filled up with God himself. Ephesians 3:17-18 (TLB)

Heaven. What a wonderful place for us to look forward to!

May God richly bless you as you move forward in His love.

> *So we do not look at what we can see right now, the troubles all around us, but we look forward to the joys in heaven which we have not yet seen. The troubles will soon be over, but the joys to come will last forever.*
>
> 2 CORINTHIANS 4:18

CLOSING THOUGHTS

You saw me before I was born.
Every day of my life was recorded in your book.
Every moment was laid out
before a single day had passed.

Isaiah 139:16 (NLT)

CHOCOLATE CHIP COOKIES

This story is at the end of the book because it deals with the darker side of life. It concerns subjects parents may want to filter for younger children.

Lord, you know everything there is to know about me.
You perceive every movement of my heart and soul,
and you understand my every thought before it even enters my mind.
You are so intimately aware of me, Lord.
You read my heart like an open book
and you know all the words I'm about to speak
before I even start a sentence!
You know every step I will take before my journey even begins.

Psalm 139:1-4 (TPT)

It's Not Just a Cookie, It's a Relationship.

Cookies—chocolate chip. I love chocolate chip cookies. My grandmother baked them. Never had a better cookie since Nana. Never! Life changed when I ate them. Life went from terror to calm. In those times it would take more than one cookie . . . Lots more!

My childhood was at best, dark. Filled with hate, anger, violence, molestations, rape, and shame. I woke up most days in fear. At 5 years old I became an adult.

The war of my childhood is over. I have come home. How did I get here? Chocolate chip cookies. I would eat them and life seemed more manageable. I could pretend that my life was normal, whatever that meant.

The boy across the street told me he would give me candy if I would come over. I came over. He laughed at me and began to molest me. I screamed. I was not so affectionately called "Foghorn," meaning I was pretty loud.

He shouted, "Get out of here you loud-mouthed bitch. If you say anything to anyone I will kill you and your family."

I ran home, turned on "Captain Kangaroo," and tearfully ate all morning. Didn't tell Mom. Actually, I was more afraid of her than of what he would do.

Mom was tough. A victim of generational abuse, she used alcohol, cigarettes, food, and anger to cope. The irony is, even though she had lived in hell as a child, her love of the Lord remained. She never felt comfortable in church, yet she made sure my sister and I attended. The plaque with John 3:16 on her bedroom wall is one of my fondest memories.

Fast forward 23 years, or so. I was 65 pounds overweight . . . a whole lot of cookies. A friend mentioned that if I wanted to lose weight a self-help program was the best way to do it. I didn't know what to expect, but I went, listened, and kept coming back.

I went from being nervous about making coffee for the meetings to volunteering for other tasks that were suggested. I learned to give away what I had received, to help myself by helping others.

Ultimately, I ended up being Chairman of the Board of Trustees and traveled nation-wide, sharing my story of how God masterminded my recovery. I was honest, kind of funny, and didn't filter what brought me to a normal weight. Folks laughed, cried, and seemed to recover with me.

I was asked to lead a retreat in Canada. There, I shared my innermost feelings about my life which had been tragic, funny at times, and despite all, filled with the love of God.

At the end of the retreat, a lovely woman approached me with a drawing. It was a beautiful sketch of the scenery outside the window of the retreat house. She told me she had quit drawing after she had been gang-raped. She believed she had lost her soul. She wanted to give me the drawing in appreciation for helping her unlock the door to her recovery and freedom.

Perhaps God had made me for a "moment like this." Who would have known that a little girl who was raped would grow up, share her story, and help change the life of an artist? God Knew.

Today, I believe God knew my grandmother would be the best cookie maker in the world for His little girl who used food to feel loved. He also knew that another of His children in Canada would be helped by my story.

I don't remember the woman's name, haven't had contact with her for over 30 years. God knows her name; He had a plan, before we were born, to bring us together at that retreat.

There are still times I weep. At times I want to jump into a bag of chocolate chippers, and yes, I still have fears. But I know God reads my heart like an open book, and He will gather all my tears.

You keep track of all my sorrows. You have collected all my tears in your bottle. You have recorded each one in your book. Psalm 56:8

In a sense, aren't we all kind of addicted? The coping mechanisms we choose can diminish our awareness of God. It's hard to hear God's voice when our internal voice is crying out for more food (chocolate-chippers), alcohol, drugs, sex, power, or control. The only healing addiction, it turns out, is being addicted to God's love.

Blessings,
Your friends in Christ,
Don & Bon

ACKNOWLEDGMENTS

Family, friends, & business associates

Dawn Egan, Ted Egan, Shayna Gregg, John Wyatt, Patti Wetmore, Erin Mecham, Sharon Wetmore, Sean Wetmore, Trevor Mecham, Dorothy Bird, Charlie Taggart, Barb Notko, Terry Notko, Bennye Rose, Christina Tostado, Dewi Susanti, Kris Sunarto, Hope Sunarto, Emily Sunarto, Marsha Yoho, Melanie Cuddy, Ariel Yow, Laura Reisiger, Captain Williams, Leslie Bass, Larry Bass, Ben Livesay, Matt Rhoads, Lisa Rhoads, Barbara Wilson, Joe Simpson, Martha Gregg, Pat Lawrence, Hilda Gallardo, Dolores Barragan, Nancy Italia, Svetlana Oppegisano, Tracy Leyvas, James Christy, Mary Peterson, Eiko Murakami, Mary Turkopp, Cindy Aiken, Sylvia Lawson, Shirley Davis, Luise Schneider, Haydee Tello, Ann Macha, Joyce Leigler, Tom Leigler, Bobbie Lewis, Margie Nakanishi, and the rest of the staff and residents at Park Terrace Assisted Living.

Alice Williams, Edward H. Sennott, Sr., Edward H. Sennott, Jr., Eleanor Sennott, Shirley Sennott, Patricia Greer, Scott Greer, E. Thomas Sennott, Carol Sennott, Jeannie Sennott, Darrin Sennott, John Sennott, Nina Sennott, Sierra Sennott, Savannah Sennott, Clayton Sennott, Tim Sennott, Terry Sennott, Christine Theobald, Tom Williams, Donna Deem, Jim Williams, Gloria McCann, Bill Williams, Sara Williams, Kay Jeffrey, Darryl Derk, Mike Lovings, Celia Stockett, John Stockett, Shari Greer, Dawn Greg, Vicki Hoskins, Billy Sands, Bobby Doolin, Howard K. Riley, Jr., Norman Tennenbaum, Portia Ware, Mary Bowsher, Staff Sergeant Geesy, Tom Brady, John DaGrosa, Jon Larsen, John Locke, Anthony Faulk, Steve Levitt, Robert Ureno, Katie Ureno, Maurice O'Link, Nick Salmela, Len Kranser, Herb Wainer, Scott Lehner, Bob Miller, Jim Williams, Linda Terry, Keith Bonchek, Ken Dembowski, Caroll

Dembowski, Bob Palocsay, Jill Palocsay, Dave Methe, Linda Methe, Rand Tanner, Cindy Tanner, Kevin Raney, Michael Farino, Kelly Farino, and our neighbors who bring us chocolate chip cookies.

Spiritual leaders

Dr. Billy Graham, Adrian Rogers, J. Vernon McGee, Charles Swindoll, R.C. Sproul, David Jeremiah, Rev. Hugh Mace, Sr., Rev. John Porter, Rev. Richard Andersen, Dr. Hugh Ross, Paul Reyes, Angie Reyes, Rev. Dan Carroll, Mike McKinney, Kristi McKinney, Pastor Randy Steele, Pastor Emily McColl, Dr. Binh Vu, Pastor Michael Johnson, Pastor Bill March, Pastor John Kano, Pastor Rick Warren, Pastor Buddy Owen, Pastor Tom Holliday, Betty Hopkins, Joan McConville, Susie Schaefer, the volunteers in the Saddleback Church Assisted Living Ministry and all those wonderful people who have hugged us and prayed for us over the years.

Christian radio, especially the music on KLOVE 107.5 FM and the broadcast team on KBRITE 740 AM.

Our sincere apologies to anyone whom we may have overlooked.

RESOURCES

AMP	Amplified® Bible, The Lockman Foundation
CEV	Contemporary English Version, American Bible Society
ICB	International Children's Bible, Thomas Nelson Bibles
KJV	King James Version
Mounce	Mounce Reverse-Interlinear New Testament, Robert H. Mounce and William D. Mounce
NASB	New American Standard Bible®, The Lockman Foundation
NIV	The Holy Bible, New International Version®, Zondervan Bible Publishing House
NKJV	New King James Version, Thomas Nelson, Inc.
NLT	The Holy Bible, New Living Translation, Tyndale House Foundation
The Message	The Message, Eugene H. Peterson
TLB	The Living Bible, Tyndale House Publishers
TPT	The Passion Translation, Broad Street Publishing®

PHOTO ATTRIBUTIONS

The photos listed below are in the public domain from the archives of the Library of Congress in Washington DC. All photos not listed below are the exclusive property of the author and retain all author rights.

SUGGESTED READING

All Things New: Heaven, Earth, and the Restoration of Everything You Love by J. Eldredge

Before Amen: The Power of a Simple Prayer by Max Lucado

Beyond the Cosmos by Hugh Ross

Bonhoeffer: Pastor, Martyr, Prophet, Spy by Eric Metaxas

Charging the Human Battery by Mac Anderson

Choose Joy Devotional: Finding Joy No Matter What You're Going Through by Kay Warren

Edging God Out by Richard J. Hart

Everybody, Always: Becoming Love in a World Full of Setbacks and Difficult People by Bob Goff

Fathered by God: Learning What Your Dad Could Never Teach You by John Eldredge

God Loves You: He Always Has--He Always Will by David Jeremiah

Gorilla Mindset by Mike Cernovich

How to Win Friends and Influence People by Dale Carnegie

Improving Your Serve by Charles Swindoll

In His Own Words by Jerry B. Jenkins

Jesus Calling: Enjoying Peace in His Presence (Jesus Calling®) by Sarah Young

Jesus: A Pilgrimage by James Martin

Killing Jesus: A History (Bill O'Reilly's Killing Series) by Bill O'Reilly

Knowing Scripture by R. C. Sproul

Love Does: Discover a Secretly Incredible Life in an Ordinary World by Bob Goff

Made for Goodness: And Why This Makes All The Difference by Desmond Tutu

Make Your Bed: Little Things That Can Change Your Life . . . And Maybe the World by William H. McRaven

Miracles: What They Are, Why They Happen, and How They Can Change Your Life by Eric Metaxas

Move Ahead with Possibility Thinking by Robert H. Schuller

My Utmost for His Highest by Oswald Chambers

Nearing Home: Life, Faith, and Finishing Well by Billy Graham

Random Acts of Kindness by Dete Meserve Rachael Greco

Reimagining the Way You Relate to God by Skye Jethani

Seeing the Unseen, Expanded Edition: A 90-Day Devotional to Set Your Mind on Eternity by Randy Alcorn

The Bait of Satan by John Bevere

The Case for Christ by Lee Strobel

The Gentle Art of Verbal Self Defense by Suzette Haden Elgin

The Harvest by John David Krygelski

The Hiding Place by Corrie Ten Boom

The Purpose Driven Church by Rick Warren

The Pursuit of God by A.W. Tozer by A.W. Tozer

The Rational Bible: Exodus by Dennis Prager

The Reason for God: Belief in an Age of Skepticism by Timothy Keller

Uninvited: Living Loved When You Feel Less Than, Left Out, and Lonely by Lysa TerKeurst

What on Earth Am I Here For? Purpose Driven Life by Rick Warren

ABOUT THE AUTHORS

DON AND BONNIE SENNOTT

In 2010, Don was a volunteer at the Water of Life Community Church food bank in Fontana, California. Loading and unloading groceries was his principal task. One afternoon, he happened to be listening to the message that one of the volunteers was giving to the people who had come to get food when he was nudged (he believes by the Holy Spirit) to ask the manager if he could also speak to the group.

She encouraged him to prepare something for the next week. The next week he gave the message, and the next, and the next. When he realized that many of the people who came for help had limited English, he started working with a translation program to prepare the talk in both English and Spanish. The only Spanish he knew was what he had picked up studying *Spanish for Dummies* and other texts. It wasn't exactly the smoothest translation, but somehow the message got across and was appreciated. Don became hooked on writing for God's people.

Bonnie came into his life compliments of eHarmony. He was smitten on the first date and remains so today. They honeymooned in Israel.

Bonnie brought her heart for Jesus to Don's writing. The two of them became serious about scriptural-based writing after they became deacons at Laguna Niguel Presbyterian Church. Several of their "Deaconese" were homebound, so Don and Bonnie started writing sermon summaries to help the shut-ins feel more a part of the congregation.

After about three years, they made the decision to start attending Saddleback Church but felt an obligation to continue serving those who had gotten used to receiving their summaries. They started putting out weekly messages based on their life experiences. Many of the pages in this book came from those stories.

At Saddleback Church, Don and Bonnie were exposed to the ideas and the writing style of Rick Warren. Several of the stories in this book reflect Pastor Warren's influence. They also became involved in the Assisted Living Ministry, acting as hosts with a team of volunteers for weekly chapel services at Park Terrace.

Don has two sons, Darrin and John, and three grandchildren, Sierra, Savannah, and Clayton.

Don is a 1970 graduate of the University of Maryland.

Bonnie served as the Program Director for the Overeaters Rehabilitation Program at the former Long Beach Naval Hospital. She was also the Chairman of the Board of an international self-help organization.

A new chapter in the book of Bonnie's life was opened fifteen years ago when she heard her daughter sing the Christian song "Open the Eyes of My Heart, Lord." She always loved Jesus, but that song made her want to know him in a deeper way.

Bonnie's daughter Dawn is an Attorney ad Litem in Arkansas. Bonnie has a terrific granddaughter, Shayna Gregg.